GREAT LAKE Effects

Buffalo Beyond Winter and Wings

A Cookbook
by
The Junior League
of Buffalo

On The Cover

Summer Paradise

22" x 30"

Corporation Collection

"An ideal summer day! Filling a space in a beautiful way, that's the artist's responsibility. A subject must stand on its own. Visually it has got to be an attention grabber, a jewel that stands out and glistens."

Margaret M. Martin, AWS

The City of Buffalo's waterfront serves not only as a source of commerce, but also as a source of recreation. During the summer months, Lake Erie and the Niagara River are filled with sailboats and sailors on a Wednesday night race or people picnicking on the beaches and in the parks during the weekends.

The Erie Basin Marina is the centerpiece of Buffalo's waterfront. From an aerial view, the Marina takes on the unique shape of a bison. The Buffalo Lighthouse that was built in 1833 is the oldest building on the waterfront today. In 1961, the Lighthouse was saved from demolition by preservationists and the Buffalo and Erie County Historical Society. In 1987, The Junior League of Buffalo members voted to donate funds to the Buffalo Lighthouse project for further lighting and structural renovations.

"Reaching Out" Statement

The Junior League of Buffalo, Inc. reaches out to women of all races, religions, and national origins who demonstrate an interest in and a commitment to voluntarism.

Mission Statement

The Junior League of Buffalo is an organization of women committed to promoting voluntarism, developing the potential of women, and to improving the community through the effective action and leadership of trained volunteers. Its purpose is exclusively educational and charitable.

Dedication

Great Lake Effects is dedicated to those individuals committed to improving the quality of life in their communities. These volunteers of yesterday, today, and tomorrow give untiringly of their efforts, energy, and enthusiasm.

Published by The Junior League of Buffalo, Inc.

Copyright© 1997 The Junior League of Buffalo, Inc.
45 Elmwood Avenue
Buffalo, New York 14201
716-882-7520

Library of Congress Catalog Number: 97-060101

ISBN: 0-9655935-0-9

Edited, Designed, and Manufactured by:

Favorite Recipes® Press
P.O. Box 305142
Nashville, Tennessee 37230
1-800-358-0560

Manufactured in the United States of America
First Printing: 10,000 copies
Second Printing: 10,000 copies

Additional copies of this book may be obtained by writing:
The Junior League of Buffalo, Inc.
45 Elmwood Avenue
Buffalo, New York 14201

This cookbook is a collection of favorite recipes, which are not necessarily original recipes. Liberties have been taken to ensure consistency of form.

The proceeds realized from the sale of *Great Lake Effects: Buffalo Beyond Winter and Wings* will be returned to the community through projects supported by The Junior League of Buffalo, Inc.

Introduction

Great Lake effects . . . impact the Buffalo weather scene first and foremost, and thus every facet of life in Western New York and the surrounding environs. Our seasonal diversity is a calling card for a variety of sportsmen, whether it be those who participate from their armchairs or on the fields, on the slopes, or on the waterways. These events have generated a need for the production of a mosaic of cuisines to suit every kind of weather condition or circumstance, both informal and formal. The cultural draw to the area beckons from a number of local theaters, the Buffalo Philharmonic Orchestra, and various historical, science, and art museums. The local ethnicity displays itself in a myriad of homes and restaurants as families and patrons gather to celebrate holidays, important events, openings, and galas. The area's food is the thread that stitches the patchwork of all these happenings together, fashioning one brightly colored cloth used to display a countless number of dishes.

Due to the shallowness of Lake Erie, storms crop up quickly and weather changes are abrupt. As a result, those who live on the lake's shores are undaunted by these transitions and carry on in spite of them, always with an alternate plan in mind. That is why Western New Yorkers, appreciating every serendipitous moment of sunshine, are always ready at short notice to pack a picnic hamper and make way to the sandy beaches and resorts along both the New York and Canadian shores. Once there, they can relax on board a sailboat or a beach blanket or head for a park to attend an outdoor concert or play. Then, as the leaves turn and autumn arrives, drives in the country to view fall's colors, and crisp afternoons of football, summon people with these same baskets of plenty to tailgate on roadsides and in parking lots. Frosty afternoons on the slopes and on the ice to entice the skier, skater, or angler, call for hot chocolate, mulled wines, and savory soups. Then suddenly the thaw comes; as springs rolls into the area and skis are stowed away for another season, the foods start to cool down and the cycle begins again. Thus Western New Yorkers never tire of the grand palate of simple and fancy gourmet delights available to them . . . all as a result of our proximity to the Great Lakes.

"Part of the secret of success in life is to eat what you like and let the food fight it out inside."

Mark Twain

The Junior League of Buffalo

The Junior League of Buffalo, Inc. is an organization of volunteers at the forefront of positive community change in the Western New York area. Since its inception on June 5, 1919, at the home of Mrs. Seymour M. Knox and under the leadership of Mrs. Nelson Taylor, the fledgling group of sixty-seven women has grown into the dynamic organization it is today, ever responding to the diverse nature of its members and the varied needs of the community which it serves.

◆ In the 1920s ◆

Recognizing the need to provide Depression Era families with quality used clothing and goods, the League purchased a Thrift Shop for $1.00 in January of 1921. Buffalo has the proud distinction of being the home of the very first League shop in the country—setting the standard in every city where a Junior League shop is located today. The League also operated a food store on Allen Street, with meals prepared and served by members for the area residents.

Proceeds from the Thrift Shop and variety shows resulted in donations to Children's Hospital totaling $37,086. The largest single donation of the twenties, $15,241, was made specifically for a Dental Clinic Endorsement Fund at Children's Hospital.

◆ In the 1930s ◆

As the membership grew in numbers, so did the scope of our work. League members were called upon to provide transportation for visiting nurses assisting at the Children's Hospital Dental Clinic. The Thrift Shop and the food store continued to operate on Allen Street. In 1938, Adam Meldrum & Anderson began over fifty years of underwriting the Junior League of Buffalo's newsletter. Our volunteers brought theater to over 2,500 area schoolchildren with a production of *Sleeping Beauty*. Fund-raising efforts paid the salary of a visiting teacher for homebound children and supported a health care clinic on Elk Street.

◆ In the 1940s ◆

The Junior League's focus broadened beyond the immediate needs of children and encompassed the arts as well. League Headquarters opened its doors as a gallery for local artists and proudly displayed a number of their works. The Junior League sponsored a Community Radio Institute lecture series and, in 1945, began a children's series entitled "Books Bring Adventure" on WEBR radio. In 1949, the doors of the Cerebral Palsy Young Adult Center were opened. The center, one of the first in the country, was established with the help and dedicated efforts of League volunteers. Funding in the 1940s went to the purchase of war bonds, to the Red Cross Blood Bank, Children's Hospital, and the Buffalo Philharmonic Orchestra.

◆ In the 1950s ◆

With a continued focus on children, the League branched into educational entertainment with puppetry and the Children's Theater. Additional funds were raised for the purchase of station wagons for the Cerebral Palsy Center. As in decades past, a great deal of time and resources went to the Children's Hospital of Buffalo. Through League support, a snack bar was opened and moneys raised went toward a new laboratory for the hospital's Pediatric Cardiac Department. The

League established the Council of Social Agencies in 1956 to act as a clearinghouse between clubs, service organizations, and other groups looking for ways of serving community health and welfare agencies. The League also sponsored philharmonic concerts for Buffalo high school students.

◆ In the 1960s ◆

"The Follies," musical reviews performed by the League members and their spouses, continued as an effective way to raise funds. While maintaining its interest in children and children's health issues, the League's work included projects in diverse areas. In 1962, after two years of planning and financial support, the "Street of 1870" exhibit opened at the Buffalo & Erie County Historical Society. In 1969, the Junior League of Buffalo celebrated its 50th Anniversary with a pledge of $50,000 to the Theodore Roosevelt Inaugural Site Foundation. This spearheaded a drive to restore the Wilcox Mansion. At this time, the League was participating in seventeen cultural, educational, and charitable projects in Western New York. Members served as guides at the Historical Society, Albright-Knox Art Gallery, and the Buffalo Museum of Science. The Junior League branched into the media as researchers, producers, and writers for educational television programs such as "Talk of the Town." Members also provided a vision-screening service for nursery school children, prepared large-print reading material for people with impaired vision, and worked with the Volunteer Service Bureau of Buffalo and the Children's Aid Society.

◆ In the 1970s ◆

Programs for women at the Erie County Correctional Facility were the focal point of a major criminal justice initiative. These successful programs received national recognition and were cited as a national model.

Concern for the environment and related issues prompted the Junior League to provide a grant of $8,500 to develop the Environmental Clearinghouse Organization. The League also co-sponsored the successful exhibit "Mirrors, Motors, and Motion" at the Albright-Knox Art Gallery. Moneys were also directed toward agencies serving children in crisis, namely Compass House and the Day Care Council of Erie County. The Thrift Shop continued to thrive in the 1970s, and Haunted Houses also served as a fund raiser. The newly created Theater of Youth Company came to fruition with the assistance of the Junior League of Buffalo. The League began to take a nonpartisan political role by issuing position statements in areas of priority concerning children's issues, health issues, arts preservation, and the environment. The first annual Ethnic Heritage Festival took place in the spring of 1979 and was located in the new Buffalo Convention Center.

◆ In the 1980s ◆

Continuing its emphasis on women and children, the League developed and supported programs such as: The Domestic Violence Coalition, Effective Parenting Information for Children, Inc., Haven House, The Community Dispute Program, The Victim Witness Program, and The Juvenile Mediation Project.

The Junior League Decorators' Show House, in partnership with *The Buffalo News*, began in 1981 with the transformation of the Larkin House into a showcase of local design talent. Proceeds from this event went to the Endowment for the ➤

...An Historical Perspective

Waterfront Performing Arts Series at LaSalle Park. The Show House event continued biannually throughout this decade, raising money for contributions to various community projects. League members focused on a new area of interest—downtown revitalization. The 1983, 1985, 1987, and 1989 Show Houses funded the following projects respectively: Cybernetic Light Show in Lafayette Square; Central Referral Service, Inc.; restoration of the Buffalo Lighthouse; and Tifft Nature Preserve Education Center.

Training, advocacy, and collaboration were also the focus of the 1980s. The League moved into its current headquarters at 45 Elmwood Avenue. Support for working women was recognized through a large grant to the Western New York Child Care Coalition for the Toy and Equipment Lending Library. In addition, the Junior League, working in collaboration with the Chamber of Commerce, developed Leadership Buffalo—a comprehensive training program for leaders in the Western New York area.

◆ In the 1990s ◆

Faced with a growing crisis of substance abuse, our League designed and developed Co-Care, a drop-in child care facility for children of alcoholic parents. This nationally recognized pilot project, housed at Buffalo General Hospital, directly responds to the needs of families in our community. "Buffalo Beckons," an access guide for the disabled, was created by League members for the community. After seventy years in existence, the Junior League Thrift Shop continues to play a vital role in the downtown community as well as to provide major funds for League-sponsored projects. The 1991 McLean House raised $90,000 for the Buffalo Zoo, and another $57,000 was provided for the continued success of League-initiated projects. The 1993 Show House, The Birtches, raised $180,000 for the Hospice Educational Center and provided funds for the continuation of the Waterfront Concert Series. Show House 1995, E. B. Green's Robert Donner Home, raised over $240,000 for Kleinhans Music Hall kitchen restoration, the Waterfront Concert Series, and additional community projects.

In this decade the Junior League also introduced its LEAF (Learning, Empowerment and Families) initiative to address the needs of economically and educationally at-risk families. A myriad of programs were designed to combat illiteracy and empower women to become self-sufficient, contributing members of society. As a result of this work in family literacy, our League was invited to participate in the United Nations' NGO Conference in Vienna, Austria, and again at the United Nations' Fourth World Conference on Women in Beijing, China. These presentations marked the first time that an individual league had its projects showcased at the international level. Additionally, the Junior League of Buffalo received the AJLI BMW Community Impact Merit Award, "Strengthening Our Communities for Families."

The League's newest endeavor, *Great Lake Effects: Buffalo Beyond Winter and Wings*, was developed to generate additional funding for the Junior League of Buffalo's community projects. It provides an awareness of what Western New York has to offer, captivates the taste buds, and pleases the eye with beautiful art work provided by local watercolorist Margaret M. Martin, AWS. Enjoy!

Table of *CONTENTS*

About the Artist

Margaret M. Martin, AWS

Born in Buffalo, New York, Margaret resides and maintains a studio in the area. She is a graduate of Boston University, has a B.F.A. degree, and is the recipient of many national watercolor awards. She is a full-time painter in the watercolor medium as well as an invited guest instructor for North American watercolor seminars and juror for national and regional exhibitions.

An elected signature member of the American Watercolor Society, National Watercolor Society, Midwest Watercolor Society, Knickerbocker Artists USA, and others, Margaret has had her works included in many corporate, private, and public collections, including the Taiwan Art Institute Museum in Taipei, Taiwan. She is listed in *Who's Who in American Art*. Her work is published in numerous books and publications.

Artist's Statement

As an artist, I organize and translate my attitudes, energies, vision, and knowledge into a statement. That translation is transferred to you to interpret in your way. A strong relationship is thus formed between creator and audience. This relationship is what a painting is about. Enjoy these reproductions! I hope you are enriched with my spirit of pride.

I paint what I know and experience and to know to see takes time. A stage is set in Western New York and comes to life in a burst of excitement and drama throughout the year. The many moods and movements, the beauty and grandeur, and the relationship of light and dark contrasts found in the area are invigorating and stimulating inspiration.

There is a tremendous emotional involvement, concentration, and patience in creating a watercolor painting. Of all the thinking and studies made in sketchbooks, only a small percentage evolve into a finished painting. My approach is a language of decent drawing, solid composition, strong abstract design shapes, light and dark value patterns, clean and rich color, an expressed mood as well as strong technical control of medium. I try to motivate visual excitement in my subject and look for an expressive and imaginative viewpoint. Every painting is a never ending challenge.

"O, Come quickly, I am drinking stars!"

Dom Perignon upon the discovery of Champagne

Bountiful
BEGINNINGS

Springtime Flourish
30" x 22"

*"Flowers in watercolor are special
to me. I aim for spontaneity,
immediacy, lushness, fresh jewel
colors and light. Rhythms are
created. Petals overlap, twist, turn
and create intriguing patterns
. . . color extraordinaire!"*
M.M.M.

The Buffalo and Erie County
Botanical Gardens was part
of the Frederick Law Olmsted Parks,
Buffalo Park and Parkway System,
plan but was actually designed and
built by the greenhouse firm of Lord
and Burnham in the late 1800s. When
touring the exquisite gardens, visitors
will find species of plants that include
bromeliads, orchids, cacti and rain
forest flora and fauna. The Gardens
give you a feeling of springtime all
through the year.

Winging Up Washington Street
22" x 30"   Private Collection

"Stop and look! One needs to see the whole—not superficial parts. I am excited with the pattern of light and shade that flows across the architecture—visual vitality! Living and working in the city has afforded me many opportunities to observe and study the urban scene." MMM

As one drives or walks Washington Street, it is hard to miss the Niagara Mohawk Building that was built in 1912 as the General Electric Tower. It is rumored that when it was built, the architectural firm of Esenwein and Johnson tried to capture the configuration of the Pharaoh's lighthouse that stood at Alexandria, Egypt. The traveler who continues down Washington Street will notice a revitalization of the area including many buildings, such as the Market Arcade, Marine Midland Arena, and North Americare Park.

Salute to Soldiers and Sailors
22" x 30"

"White paper can invigorate a painting with energy. The medium forces me to save and organize the whites. The monument design is strong and powerful. The painting statement should be strong as well." MMM

The Soldiers and Sailors Monument located in Lafayette Square was built in 1882 in memory of those soldiers who served in the Civil War. Also located in Lafayette Square is the Cybernetic Light Theater. Proceeds from the 1983 and 1985 Junior League of Buffalo and *The Buffalo News* Decorators' Show Houses provided the means to turn on the lights in this square and give people a reason to come downtown.

Bountiful
BEGINNINGS

*The Buffalo slogan
"City of Good
Neighbors" was coined
in 1940.*

Elegant Artichoke Appetizer

4 ounces saltine crackers,
finely crushed

1 (12-ounce) jar marinated
artichoke hearts

1 medium onion, finely
chopped

1½ teaspoons minced garlic

9 eggs, lightly beaten

1¾ cups grated Parmesan
cheese

◆ Pat the cracker crumbs evenly into a
greased 10x15-inch baking pan.

◆ Drain the artichokes, reserving the
liquid. Chop the artichokes.

◆ Sauté the onion and garlic in the
reserved liquid in a skillet until tender.

◆ Mix the onion mixture, artichokes,
eggs and cheese in a bowl. Spoon
over the prepared layer.

◆ Bake at 350 degrees for 25 to 30
minutes.

◆ Makes 10 to 15 servings.

Artichoke Pepper Pizza

1 medium red bell pepper

1 teaspoon olive oil

2 cloves of garlic, crushed

¼ cup light mayonnaise

⅛ teaspoon red pepper

⅛ teaspoon black pepper

1 cup artichoke hearts

1 (1-pound) Boboli pizza
crust

1 cup shredded mozzarella
cheese

½ cup crumbled feta cheese

½ teaspoon thyme

◆ Cut the red bell pepper into strips.
Sauté in the olive oil in a skillet for
3 minutes. Stir in half the garlic. Sauté
for 1 minute.

◆ Process the remaining garlic, mayonnaise, red pepper, black pepper and
artichokes in a food processor until the
artichokes are finely chopped.

◆ Place the pizza crust on a baking
sheet. Spread with the artichoke
mixture to within ½ inch of the edge.
Top with the red bell pepper. Sprinkle
with the mozzarella cheese, feta cheese
and thyme.

◆ Bake at 450 degrees for 14 minutes.

◆ Makes 4 servings.

Chicken Pesto Pizza

8 ounces boneless skinless
  chicken breasts

1 red bell pepper

1 (9-inch) pizza shell

¼ cup pesto

6 ounces goat cheese,
  crumbled

2 tablespoons chopped
  garlic

Dried basil, oregano and
  thyme to taste

———————◆———————

*Feta cheese is a salty
crumbly white goat cheese,
best used in salads and
Greek recipes.*

◆ Rinse the chicken and pat dry. Sauté
  the chicken in a skillet or grill the
  chicken over hot coals for several
  minutes or until almost done. Let
  stand until cool. Cut into diagonal
  strips.

◆ Grill the red pepper over hot coals or
  broil until the skin is blistered and
  charred on all sides, turning frequently.
  Place the red pepper in cold water
  until the skin is easily removed;
  discard the skin. Julienne the red
  pepper, discarding the seeds and stem.

◆ Place the pizza shell on a baking
  sheet. Spread with the pesto. Arrange
  the chicken over the pesto so that each
  wedge of pizza will have a chicken
  strip. Top with the red pepper. Sprinkle
  with a mixture of the goat cheese,
  garlic, basil, oregano and thyme.

◆ Bake at 400 to 450 degrees for 7 to 12
  minutes or until bubbly.

◆ Makes 2 servings.

*Sixteen other cities in
the United States share
the name Buffalo.*

Westside Bruschetta

1 baguette with sesame
   seeds

4 to 6 tablespoons extra-
   virgin olive oil

1 tablespoon minced garlic

1 tablespoon Romano
   cheese

¼ teaspoon ground pepper

1 red bell pepper, cut into
   ¼-inch pieces

1 yellow bell pepper, cut into
   ¼-inch pieces

2 plum tomatoes, cut into
   ¼-inch slices

3 green onions, cut into
   ¼-inch slices

½ cup shredded
   mozzarella, asiago or
   gorgonzola cheese

4 ounces mushrooms, cut
   into ⅛-inch slices

4 ounces prosciutto or
   smoked ham, cut into
   ½-inch strips

Freshly grated pecorino
   Romano cheese

---

*To mince is to cut or
chop into very small pieces,
generally less than ¼ inch
in size.*

♦ Slice the baguette lengthwise into halves. Place cut side up on a baking sheet.

♦ Combine the olive oil, garlic, 1 table-spoon Romano cheese and pepper in a bowl and mix well. Spread over the cut sides of the bread halves. Arrange the bell peppers, tomatoes and green onions on each bread half. Sprinkle with the mozzarella cheese. Top with the mushrooms and prosciutto.

♦ Bake at 350 degrees for 5 to 10 minutes or until the cheese melts.

♦ Broil for 2 to 3 minutes or just until the cheese begins to brown. Cut into 2-inch slices. Sprinkle with freshly grated pecorino Romano cheese.

♦ Makes 4 to 6 servings.

Greek Meat Pastries

¼ cup butter

1 pound ground round

2 small onions, finely chopped

2 cloves of garlic, finely chopped

1 teaspoon salt

¾ teaspoon pepper

½ teaspoon curry powder

½ teaspoon cinnamon

½ teaspoon allspice

1 (8-ounce) can tomato sauce

8 ounces phyllo pastry

Melted butter

◆ Heat ¼ cup butter in a skillet until melted. Add the ground round, onions and garlic and mix well.

◆ Cook until the onions are slightly cooked and the ground round is brown, stirring constantly. Stir in the salt, pepper, curry powder, cinnamon and allspice. Adjust the seasonings if desired. Add the tomato sauce and mix well. Bring to a boil, stirring constantly. Reduce heat.

◆ Simmer, covered, for 30 minutes or until the ground round is cooked through, stirring occasionally.

◆ Cool slightly. Drain the excess liquid.

◆ Unwrap phyllo pastry and place 1 sheet on work surface. Cover remaining phyllo with damp cloth to prevent drying out. Brush pastry with melted butter. Place second sheet of phyllo on top and brush with melted butter. Cut phyllo into 4x6-inch pieces. Place 1 teaspoon of the ground round mixture at the end of the pastry; use triangular flag folding technique to wrap meat. Brush all the sides with melted butter. Place on a baking sheet. Repeat the procedure with the remaining phyllo pastry and ground round mixture.

◆ Bake at 450 degrees for 15 minutes or until light brown. Cool slightly. Serve warm.

◆ Makes 100 meat rolls.

Smoked Chicken Salad with Endive Spears

2 ounces haricots verts or green beans

8 ounces smoked chicken or turkey, diced into ¼-inch pieces

½ red bell pepper, finely diced

1 large shallot, minced

1 tablespoon chopped fresh tarragon or 1 teaspoon dried

¼ cup olive oil

2 tablespoons white wine vinegar

¾ cup crumbled Gorgonzola cheese

3 tablespoons chopped toasted walnuts (optional)

Salt and pepper to taste

4 heads Belgian endive, separated into spears

———◆———

Dice refers to cutting into cubes about ¼ inch in size.

◆ Bring a small amount of water to a boil in a saucepan. Add the green beans.

◆ Cook for 4 minutes or until tender; drain. Cover with cold water; drain. Cut the green beans crosswise into thin slices.

◆ Combine the green beans, chicken, red pepper, shallot and tarragon in a bowl and mix well. May be prepared to this point and stored, covered, in the refrigerator for 1 day in advance.

◆ Combine the olive oil and wine vinegar in a saucepan. Bring to a simmer, swirling the pan occasionally. Stir in the cheese. Pour over the green bean mixture, tossing to coat. Stir in the walnuts. Season with salt and pepper.

◆ Chill, covered, for 30 minutes to 8 hours.

◆ Shape 2 teaspoons of the green bean mixture into a ball; press into the stem end of an endive spear. Repeat the procedure with the remaining endive spears and green bean mixture.

◆ Arrange the endive spears in a spoke formation on a serving platter.

◆ Makes 30 appetizers.

Across the Border Won Tons

8 ounces boneless skinless
chicken breast

2 large dried shiitake
mushrooms

1 (8-ounce) can water
chestnuts, drained

2 scallions

2 large cloves of garlic

2 slices peeled fresh ginger

1 tablespoon cornstarch

2 teaspoons soy sauce

2 teaspoons dry white wine
or dry vermouth

½ teaspoon kosher salt

¼ teaspoon dried red
pepper flakes

60 won ton wrappers

Vegetable oil for deep-frying

---

*Shiitake mushrooms are
easily identified by their
garlic-pine aroma. If they
are odorless, they are not
fresh. Select mushrooms
that are firm and dry with
no soft spots. Substitute
these mushrooms in any
recipe that calls for button
mushrooms.*

◆ Rinse the chicken and pat dry.

◆ Soak the mushrooms in hot water to
cover for 25 minutes or until softened.
Drain and squeeze dry. Discard the
mushroom stems.

◆ Process the mushrooms, water
chestnuts, scallions, garlic and ginger
in a food processor fitted with a metal
blade until finely chopped; do not
purée. Add the chicken, cornstarch,
soy sauce, white wine, kosher salt and
red pepper flakes. Pulse 6 to 8 times
or just until the mixture is blended.

◆ Place 1 won ton wrapper with 1
corner facing you on a dry work
surface. Spoon 1½ teaspoons of the
chicken mixture in the center of the
wrapper; moisten the edges. Fold to
form a triangle. Bring the 2 corners of
the folded edge toward the center and
press into the opposite corner to seal.
Place on a baking sheet. Repeat with
the remaining wrappers and chicken
mixture. Chill in the refrigerator.

◆ Won tons may be prepared and frozen
before frying on a baking sheet and
stored in plastic bags in the freezer.
Deep-fry straight from the freezer.

◆ Deep-fry the won tons in hot oil until
golden brown; drain. Serve with sweet-
and-sour sauce, mustard sauce, hoisin
sauce or plum sauce.

◆ Makes 60 won tons.

*Buffalo is nicknamed the
City of Good Neighbors
and the Queen City of the
Great Lakes.*

Filipino Spring Rolls (Lumpia)

2 ounces rice noodles

1 pound ground pork

2 cloves of garlic, finely chopped

1 small onion, chopped

2 medium carrots, peeled, grated

1 egg, beaten

2 tablespoons fish sauce*

2 tablespoons soy sauce*

1 teaspoon kosher salt

½ teaspoon freshly ground pepper

1 package thin spring roll wrappers*

2 tablespoons cornstarch and water paste, or 1 beaten egg yolk

3 to 4 cups peanut or vegetable oil

Oriental Sweet-and-Sour Dipping Sauce (page 21)

———◆———

*These ingredients can be purchased at an oriental market or the oriental section of your local supermarket.

◆ Bring a 3-quart saucepan of salted water to a boil. Add the rice noodles.

◆ Simmer for 8 minutes; drain. Let stand until cool. Cut the noodles into finger-length pieces.

◆ Mix the noodles, pork, garlic, onion, carrots, egg, fish sauce, soy sauce, kosher salt and pepper in a bowl.

◆ Separate the spring roll wrappers gently. Brush the edges with the cornstarch paste. Place 1 level tablespoon of the noodle mixture at the end closest to you. Shape the filling along the length of the wrapper edge; thickness should be about the size of your small finger. Fold the 2 sides over the narrow ends of the filling. Roll, making sure the sides are tucked in. The spring roll should resemble a tightly rolled cylinder.

◆ Deep-fry 4 to 6 spring rolls at a time in 350-degree oil for 6 to 8 minutes or until golden brown; drain.

◆ Arrange the spring rolls on a bed of lettuce, fresh mint, cilantro and sliced cucumbers. Serve with Oriental Sweet-and-Sour Dipping Sauce or mustard sauce.

◆ Makes 15 to 20 spring rolls.

Oriental Sweet-and-Sour Dipping Sauce

1 cup sugar

½ cup water

½ cup cider vinegar

1 tablespoon chopped fresh
    green bell pepper

1 ounce chopped pimento

2 teaspoons paprika

1 tablespoon cornstarch

2 tablespoons cold water

◆ Combine the sugar, water, cider vinegar, green pepper, pimento and paprika in a saucepan. Bring to a boil.

◆ Boil for 5 minutes, stirring occasionally. Stir in a mixture of the cornstarch and cold water.

◆ Cook until slightly thickened, stirring constantly. Let stand until cool.

◆ Chill, covered, until serving time.

◆ Makes 1 cup.

Cider vinegar has a fruity flavor and is best complemented by strong flavored herbs and spices.

Buffalo China is one of twelve potteries in the world that make fine vitreous china, which is sought by collectors today. Buffalo China supplies thousands of restaurants and hotels across the nation with tableware.

Picnic Torte

1 package puff pastry

3 large red bell peppers

2 pounds fresh spinach

5 tablespoons unsalted butter

2 tablespoons olive oil

2 medium shallots, minced

2 cloves of garlic, minced

¼ teaspoon nutmeg

Salt and pepper to taste

5 eggs

1 tablespoon minced fresh parsley

2 teaspoons minced fresh chives

1 teaspoon minced fresh tarragon

◆ Thaw the puff pastry using package directions.

◆ Place the red peppers on a baking sheet. Broil until the skin is blistered and charred on all sides, turning frequently. Place the red peppers in a paper food storage bag. Steam for 10 minutes. Peel, seed and chop the red peppers.

◆ Sauté the spinach in 2 tablespoons of the butter and olive oil in a skillet for 2 minutes. Add the shallots and garlic and mix well.

◆ Sauté for 2 minutes or until the shallots and garlic are tender. Drain; squeeze the moisture from the spinach. Season with the nutmeg, salt and pepper.

◆ Beat 5 eggs, parsley, chives, tarragon, salt and pepper in a bowl until mixed.

◆ Heat 1 tablespoon of the butter in a skillet until melted. Add ½ of the egg mixture, swirling to cover the bottom. Cook over low heat for 3 minutes or until set; turn the omelet.

◆ Cook for 1 minute longer. Remove to a plate. Heat 1 tablespoon of the butter in the skillet. Repeat the procedure with the remaining egg mixture.

◆ Rub the remaining 1 tablespoon of the butter over the side and bottom of a 9-inch springform pan.

Assembling Torte:

12 ounces Gruyère cheese
   or Swiss cheese,
   shredded

12 ounces thinly sliced
   smoked turkey or ham

1 egg, beaten

1 tablespoon water

◆ Roll ¾ of the puff pastry ¼ inch thick.
   Fit into the prepared springform pan,
   allowing extra pastry to hang over the
   rim; do not stretch the pastry. Chill for
   10 minutes.

◆ Place 1 omelet in the bottom of the
   pastry-lined pan. Layer ½ of the
   spinach, ½ of the cheese, ½ of the
   turkey and the red peppers over the
   omelet. Top with the remaining turkey,
   remaining cheese, remaining spinach
   and the remaining omelet.

◆ Roll the remaining puff pastry ¼ inch
   thick; fit on top of the prepared layers.
   Trim the overhang to ½ inch. Brush
   the top and edge of the torte with a
   mixture of 1 egg and water. May
   decorate the top with any remaining
   pieces of puff pastry.

◆ Chill for 2 to 10 hours. Place the torte
   on a baking sheet.

◆ Bake at 375 degrees for 1½ hours. To
   prevent overbrowning, cover loosely
   with foil toward end of baking process.

◆ Cool on a wire rack for 15 minutes.
   Remove sides of springform pan; slice.

◆ Makes 10 to 12 servings.

*Millard Fillmore was
the first Chancellor of the
University of Buffalo.*

Spicy Hot Shrimp

A great outdoor summer treat. Serve with baguettes to "sop" up the sauce.

1 pound unpeeled shrimp

3 slices bacon, chopped

1 cup margarine

2 tablespoons Dijon mustard

2 tablespoons crab boil herb mixture

1¼ teaspoons chili powder

1 teaspoon freshly ground pepper

¼ teaspoon basil

¼ teaspoon thyme

¼ teaspoon oregano

¼ teaspoon Tabasco sauce

3 cloves of garlic, crushed

◆ Arrange the shrimp in a shallow baking dish.

◆ Sauté the bacon in a skillet until transparent. Stir in the margarine, Dijon mustard, crab boil, chili powder, pepper, basil, thyme, oregano, Tabasco sauce and garlic.

◆ Simmer for 5 minutes, stirring occasionally. Pour over the shrimp.

◆ Bake at 375 degrees for 10 minutes; stir.

◆ Bake for 10 minutes longer or until the shrimp turn pink.

◆ Makes 2 to 4 servings.

Chili powder is made from dried red chile peppers. The taste will range from mild to fiery, depending on the type of chile used. Used primarily in Mexican cuisine, it is also delicious added to eggs, dips, and sauces.

Hot Crab au Gratin

12 to 16 ounces fresh,
  frozen or imitation crab
  meat, chopped

11 ounces cream cheese,
  softened

3 tablespoons finely
  chopped onion

1½ tablespoons milk

1½ teaspoons white
  horseradish

½ teaspoon chopped fresh
  or dried chives

½ teaspoon dried hot pepper
  flakes (optional)

½ teaspoon dillweed

Freshly ground black pepper
  to taste

Sliced Swiss cheese

Grated Parmesan cheese

Shredded Swiss cheese

◆ Combine the crab meat, cream cheese, onion, milk, horseradish, chives, hot pepper flakes, dillweed and black pepper in a bowl and mix well.

◆ Grease the bottom of a baking dish. Spread half the crab meat mixture in the prepared dish. Top with sliced Swiss cheese; sprinkle generously with Parmesan cheese. Spread with the remaining crab meat mixture; sprinkle with shredded Swiss cheese and more Parmesan cheese.

◆ Bake at 375 degrees for 30 minutes or until light brown and bubbly.

◆ Serve warm with assorted party crackers or party bread.

◆ Makes 12 to 15 servings.

Swiss cheese is known for its holes and pale yellow color. It has a sweetish, nutty flavor and is great served with fresh fruit and French bread.

Parmesan cheese is a hard, brittle, sharp cheese, light yellow in color and generally used finely grated.

The first telegraph message was received in Buffalo in 1846 sent from Albany.

Sorrento Cheese distributes a fine quality of Italian cheeses across the country.

Gouda Baguettes

8 ounces Gouda cheese, shredded

1 cup sour cream

2 tablespoons dry Italian salad dressing mix

2 baguettes, sliced, toasted

◆ Combine the cheese, sour cream and salad dressing mix in a bowl and mix well.

◆ Chill, covered, until serving time.

◆ Serve with the toasted baguette slices.

◆ Makes a variable number of servings.

Olive Pesto Spread

1 cup pitted kalamata olives

1 cup pitted domestic black olives

3 tablespoons grated pecorino Romano cheese

1 tablespoon puréed fresh garlic

1 teaspoon finely minced fresh basil

½ cup olive oil

◆ Combine the olives in a food processor container. Process until finely chopped.

◆ Combine the olives, cheese, garlic, basil and olive oil in a bowl and mix well.

◆ Chill, covered, for 2 hours. Serve with assorted party crackers and/or party breads.

◆ Makes 2 cups.

Goat Cheese with Sun-Dried Tomatoes

8 ounces goat cheese

4 ounces oil-pack sun-dried tomatoes

½ teaspoon chopped fresh basil

½ teaspoon chopped garlic

◆ Place the goat cheese in a baking dish. Bake at 300 degrees for 15 minutes.

◆ Combine the sun-dried tomatoes, basil and garlic in a bowl and mix well. Pour over the goat cheese.

◆ Serve with baguette slices or assorted party crackers.

◆ Makes 10 to 12 servings.

Salsa Spinach Dip

2 (10-ounce) packages
  frozen chopped spinach,
  thawed, drained

2 tablespoons butter

2 tablespoons flour

1 (16-ounce) can artichoke
  hearts, drained, chopped

8 ounces jalapeño cheese,
  shredded

8 ounces Romano cheese,
  grated

½ cup evaporated milk

⅛ teaspoon each garlic salt,
  celery salt and pepper

Tortilla chips, sour cream
  and salsa

◆ Squeeze the moisture from the
  spinach.

◆ Heat the butter in a saucepan until
  melted. Stir in the flour.

◆ Cook the mixture until thickened,
  stirring constantly. Add the spinach,
  artichokes, jalapeño cheese, Romano
  cheese, evaporated milk, garlic salt,
  celery salt and pepper and mix well.

◆ Cook until the cheese melts, stirring
  constantly.

◆ Spoon into a slow cooker or chafing
  dish to keep warm. Serve with tortilla
  chips, sour cream and salsa.

◆ Makes 12 servings.

Buffalo Freeze

*A fabulous summer drink for parties, relaxing by
the pool, or even cookbook meetings!*

9 cups water

2 cups dark rum

1 (12-ounce) can lemonade

1 (12-ounce) can frozen
  orange juice concentrate

3 tablespoons grenadine

1 tablespoon maraschino
  cherry juice

◆ Combine the water, rum, lemonade,
  orange juice concentrate, grenadine
  and cherry juice in a freezer container
  and mix well.

◆ Freeze to desired consistency.

◆ Makes 18 servings.

Caribbean Cocktail Punch

When you think of Caribbean Cocktail Punch, you think of summer. When you think of summer in Buffalo, you think of Crystal Beach Amusement Park. The park has since closed, but the memory lives on of Crystal Beach Suckers, the Comet Roller Coaster, and the Crystal Beach boat, The Canadiana, *which would take revellers from downtown Buffalo to the Park.*

*1 (12-ounce) can frozen
orange juice concentrate*

*1 (12-ounce) can frozen
pineapple juice
concentrate*

*1 (12-ounce) can frozen
pink lemonade
concentrate*

*1 (12-ounce) can frozen
pink grapefruit juice*

*1 quart each water and
wine*

Fresh or frozen raspberries

◆ Combine the orange juice concentrate, pineapple juice concentrate, pink lemonade concentrate, pink grapefruit juice concentrate, water and wine in a punch bowl and mix well. Stir in the raspberries.

◆ Ladle into punch cups.

◆ May substitute passion fruit juice for pink grapefruit juice.

◆ Makes 18 to 20 servings.

Orange Iced Tea

Use flavored teas to create a different twist.

3 cups boiling water

5 tea bags

1 cup sugar

5 cups cold water

1 cup orange juice

¼ cup fresh lemon juice

1 mint sprig

◆ Combine the boiling water and tea bags in a heatproof container. Let steep for 10 to 15 minutes. Remove the tea bags.

◆ Add the sugar, stirring until dissolved. Mix in the cold water, orange juice, lemon juice and mint.

◆ Chill until serving time. Pour over ice cubes in glasses.

◆ Makes 10 servings.

Broccoli Slaw

8 ounces bacon, chopped

5 pounds broccoli

1 cup sliced red onion

¼ cup golden raisins

¼ cup dark raisins

3 cups mayonnaise

1½ cups sugar

¼ cup white wine vinegar

1½ teaspoons salt

½ teaspoon pepper

◆ Fry the bacon in a skillet until crispy; drain.

◆ Separate the broccoli stems from the florets. Process the stems and onion in a food processor until shredded. Cut the florets into small pieces.

◆ Mix the florets, onion mixture, bacon and raisins in a bowl.

◆ Combine the mayonnaise, sugar, wine vinegar, salt and pepper in a bowl and mix well. Add to the broccoli mixture, stirring until mixed.

◆ Chill, covered, until serving time.

◆ Makes 30 servings.

Black Bean Salad

Serve with tortilla chips and nacho sauce for an easy low-calorie lunch.

2 (15-ounce) cans black beans, drained

2 green bell peppers, julienned

1 tomato, cut into wedges

1 red onion, finely chopped

⅓ cup olive oil

3 tablespoons lime juice

2 teaspoons chopped parsley

1 teaspoon salt

½ teaspoon red pepper flakes

◆ Combine the black beans, green peppers, tomato and onion in a bowl, stirring gently to mix.

◆ Pour a mixture of the olive oil, lime juice, parsley, salt and red pepper flakes over the bean mixture, tossing to coat.

◆ Marinate, covered, in the refrigerator for 6 hours or longer, stirring 2 to 3 times.

◆ Spoon onto a lettuce-lined serving platter.

◆ Makes 6 servings.

Nouveau Chicken Salad

This is a cookbook committee favorite! Serve on a lettuce-lined salad plate with Pear Bread Extraordinaire (page 45) and a seasonal fresh fruit salad for a delightful shower luncheon.

2 whole boneless skinless
  chicken breasts

½ cup Italian salad
  dressing

⅔ cup mayonnaise

¼ cup Dijon mustard

1 teaspoon minced fresh
  dillweed

1 teaspoon minced fresh
  chives

1 cup slivered almonds

1 cup golden raisins

♦ Rinse the chicken and pat dry. Arrange in a shallow dish. Pour the salad dressing over the chicken, turning to coat.

♦ Marinate in the refrigerator for 1 hour, turning occasionally. Drain, reserving the marinade.

♦ Grill the chicken over medium-hot coals for 12 to 15 minutes or until cooked through, turning and basting with the reserved marinade frequently. Chop into bite-size pieces when cool.

♦ Combine the mayonnaise, Dijon mustard, dillweed and chives in a bowl and mix well. Let stand for 15 to 30 minutes to allow flavors to marry.

♦ Spread the almonds in a single layer on a baking sheet.

♦ Bake at 300 degrees until light brown, turning frequently. Let stand until cool. Chop the almonds finely.

♦ Combine the chicken and mayonnaise mixture in a bowl and mix well. Stir in the almonds and raisins.

♦ Chill, covered, for 2 to 3 hours.

♦ Makes 6 servings.

Pear and Swiss Cheese Salad

2 pears, sliced

Lemon juice

¼ cup sour cream

¼ cup plain yogurt

⅛ teaspoon cardamom

⅛ teaspoon cinnamon

1 cup shredded Swiss cheese

Lettuce leaves

½ cup cashews, pecans or walnuts, roasted

◆ Place the pears in a bowl. Sprinkle with the lemon juice to prevent browning, tossing to coat.

◆ Combine the sour cream, yogurt, cardamom and cinnamon in a bowl and mix well. Add the pears and cheese, tossing gently.

◆ Chill, covered, until serving time.

◆ Spoon onto a lettuce-lined serving platter. Sprinkle with the cashews.

◆ Makes 4 servings.

Szechwan-Style Cucumbers

2 to 3 cucumbers, sliced

2 tablespoons kosher salt

9 or 10 thin garlic slices

1 tablespoon Hot Chili Oil

1 tablespoon sesame oil

2 teaspoons sugar

1 teaspoon hot bean paste

1 tablespoon cider vinegar

◆ Place the cucumbers in a bowl; sprinkle with the kosher salt.

◆ Combine the garlic, hot chili oil, sesame oil, sugar, hot bean paste and cider vinegar in a bowl and mix well. Pour over the cucumbers and mix well.

◆ Serve chilled or at room temperature.

◆ Makes 4 servings.

◆ *Prepare Hot Chili Oil by combining 1 tablespoon black peppercorns, 3 fresh or dried bay leaves, 5 small dried hot red chile peppers with seeds, 3 fresh thyme sprigs 3 to 4 inches long, and 2 cups olive oil in the order listed. Pour into a dry sterilized wine bottle; seal with a cork. Store in a cool dark environment for 2 to 3 weeks to allow the oil to be infused with the other flavors.*

Baked Brie Salad with Raspberry Vinaigrette

½ head red leaf lettuce

½ head green leaf lettuce

½ head Boston lettuce

½ head radicchio

12 to 16 spears Belgian endive

¼ to ½ cup pine nuts

1 (3-inch) wedge Brie cheese, rind removed

Raspberry Vinaigrette (below)

The greens may be prepared early in the day, rolled tightly in a towel with 1 to 2 ice cubes, and stored in the refrigerator. The Raspberry Vinaigrette may be prepared 1 day in advance and stored, covered, in the refrigerator.

◆ Rinse and dry the lettuce; tear into bite-size pieces. Rinse and dry the endive spears.

◆ Spread the pine nuts on a baking sheet. Toast at 350 degrees for 5 minutes, turning frequently.

◆ Arrange 2 endive spears on each salad plate; top with a mixture of the remaining lettuce. Sprinkle with the pine nuts.

◆ Cut the Brie cheese into six to eight ¼-inch slices. Place on a baking sheet sprayed with nonstick cooking spray.

◆ Heat at 250 degrees for 1 minute or until the cheese melts. Top each salad with 1 slice of Brie cheese. Drizzle with the Raspberry Vinaigrette.

◆ Makes 6 to 8 servings.

Raspberry Vinaigrette

10 tablespoons olive oil

4 tablespoons raspberry vinegar

¼ teaspoon pepper

½ teaspoon dry mustard

1 clove of garlic, crushed

1 teaspoon chives

◆ Whisk 4 tablespoons of the olive oil, 2 tablespoons of the raspberry vinegar, pepper and dry mustard in a bowl until mixed. Add the remaining 6 tablespoons olive oil, remaining 2 tablespoons raspberry vinegar and garlic, whisking constantly. Stir in the chives just before serving.

◆ Makes 6 to 8 servings.

Warm Goat Cheese Salad with Red Pepper Vinaigrette

2 red bell peppers

1½ cups olive oil

1 teaspoon salt

½ teaspoon freshly ground
pepper

½ teaspoon rosemary,
crushed

2 large cloves of garlic,
finely chopped

¼ to ⅓ cup white vinegar

12 ounces goat cheese

1 head red leaf lettuce

1 head romaine

1 head Boston lettuce,
separated into leaves

1 head curly endive,
separated into leaves

1 head radicchio, separated
into leaves

1 head Belgian endive,
separated into spears

◆ Cut the red peppers lengthwise into halves; discard the cores and seeds. Arrange on a baking sheet; press each half flat with the palm of your hand.

◆ Broil until charred on all sides, turning frequently. Place in a paper storage bag; seal tightly.

◆ Steam for 15 to 20 minutes. Peel and chop into ½-inch pieces.

◆ Place the roasted red peppers and any liquid that develops from the peppers in a bowl. Add the olive oil, salt, pepper, rosemary and garlic and mix well. Whisk in the white vinegar; mixture will be slightly thickened.

◆ Cut the goat cheese into ½-inch slices. Arrange in an ovenproof container.

◆ Bake at 300 degrees for 10 minutes or until heated through.

◆ Tear the red leaf lettuce into large pieces. Arrange on a serving platter, overlapping the sides of the platter. Tear the romaine and place over the red leaf lettuce. Top with the Boston lettuce. Arrange the curly endive, radicchio and Belgian endive decoratively on the platter. Top with the warm goat cheese. Whisk the dressing; drizzle over the salad. Serve immediately.

◆ Makes 8 to 10 servings.

Larry Bell leased the old Pierce-Arrow automobile plant in Buffalo to build America's first jet airplane.

Tomato and Mozzarella Pasta Salad

12 ounces farfalle or cavatelli

Salt to taste

3 tablespoons extra-virgin olive oil

2 pounds tomatoes, cored, chopped

5⅓ ounces part-skim mozzarella cheese, chopped

½ cup chopped fresh basil

¼ cup chopped red onion

3 tablespoons red wine vinegar

Freshly ground pepper to taste

Mixed salad greens, including arugula or watercress

◆ Cook the pasta in boiling salted water in a saucepan until al dente; drain. Rinse in cool water; drain. Combine the pasta and 1 tablespoon of the olive oil in a bowl, tossing to coat.

◆ Combine the remaining 2 tablespoons olive oil, tomatoes, cheese, basil, onion and wine vinegar in a bowl and mix gently. Season with salt and pepper.

◆ Arrange the salad greens on individual salad plates.

◆ Toss the pasta with the tomato mixture in a bowl. Spoon over the salad greens. Garnish with grated pecorino Romano cheese.

◆ Makes 4 to 6 servings.

Extra-virgin olive oil, fruity in flavor and green in color, is made from the first cold pressing of olives and is best used in salads. Virgin olive oil is more suitable for cooked dishes and sauces, and has a lighter golden color. There is no substitute for olive oil . . . it is well worth investing in a quality brand.

Layered Salad

1 pound spinach, stems removed, torn into bite-size pieces

2 teaspoons (about) salt

2 teaspoons (about) sugar

½ teaspoon (about) pepper

1 pound bacon, crisp-fried, crumbled

6 hard-cooked eggs, chopped

1 head iceberg lettuce, torn into bite-size pieces

5 ounces fresh or frozen baby peas

1 small Bermuda onion, thinly sliced

2 cups mayonnaise

8 ounces Jarlsberg cheese, julienned

◆ Place the spinach in a 10-inch glass bowl. Sprinkle with 1 teaspoon of the salt, 1 teaspoon of the sugar and ¼ teaspoon of the pepper. Layer with the bacon and eggs, extending each layer to touch the side of the bowl.

◆ Arrange the lettuce over the prepared layers. Sprinkle with the remaining 1 teaspoon salt, remaining 1 teaspoon sugar and remaining ¼ teaspoon pepper.

◆ Layer with the peas and onion. Spread with the mayonnaise and top with the cheese.

◆ Chill, covered, for 12 to 24 hours.

◆ Makes 8 to 10 servings.

Kleinhans Music Hall

Kleinhans Music Hall was constructed during the Depression with bequests of about one million dollars from the Kleinhans family, longtime Buffalo clothing merchants. The hall is constructed in the shape of a violin or cello with the two lobes of the instrument housing concert auditoriums.

Although acoustically superb, the main performance hall is almost extremely plain, probably to keep the audience from being diverted from the music.

Kleinhans Music Hall is the home of the Buffalo Philharmonic Orchestra.

Lemon Ginger Rice Salad

3 cups cooked brown rice

1½ cups cooked wild rice

2 bunches green onions, chopped

1 red bell pepper, chopped

1 yellow bell pepper, chopped

1 (10-ounce) package frozen green peas

½ cup slivered almonds

½ cup walnut pieces

¾ cup olive oil

½ cup vegetable oil

Juice of 2 lemons

1 tablespoon ginger powder, or to taste

Salt and pepper to taste

◆ Combine the brown rice, wild rice, green onions, red pepper, yellow pepper, peas, almonds and walnuts in a bowl and mix well.

◆ Combine the olive oil, vegetable oil, lemon juice, ginger powder, salt and pepper in a jar with a lid, shaking to blend.

◆ Pour over the rice salad, tossing to coat. Serve immediately.

◆ Makes 10 to 12 servings.

Raspberry Poppy Seed Vinaigrette

1 cup vegetable oil

½ cup sugar

⅓ cup raspberry vinegar

1 teaspoon salt

1 teaspoon poppy seeds

1 teaspoon mustard

◆ Combine the oil, sugar, raspberry vinegar, salt, poppy seeds and mustard in a cruet, shaking to mix.

◆ Drizzle over fresh greens and garnish with sautéed pecans and/or fresh raspberries.

◆ Makes 1½ cups.

Sweet & Savory SIDES

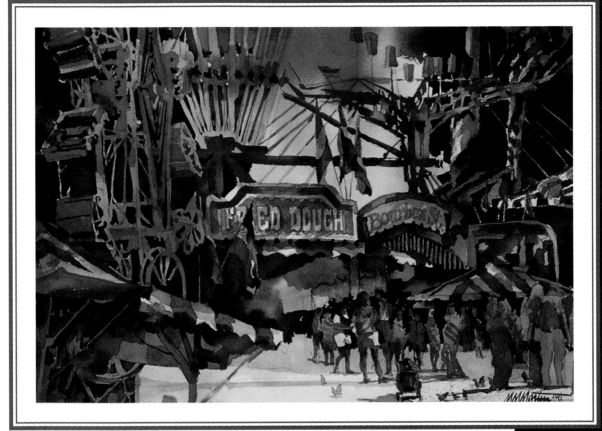

Friendship Festival
19" x 27"   Private Collection

"A kaleidoscope of good company and crescendo. It was the razzle-dazzle that attracted me to this colorful whirl of activity. I aim for rich color."   MMM

Since its beginning in 1987, the Friendship Festival annually commemorates the July 1, 1867 birth of Canada and the July 4, 1776 anniversary of the signing of the Declaration of Independence. Held in the shadow of the Peace Bridge that connects the two nations, the celebration in Fort Erie is set in Mather Park, named after Alonzo Mather, a U.S. citizen who championed the friendship of the two nations and proposed the building of the bridge. In Buffalo the festival is held in LaSalle Park, which houses the Waterfront Pavilion, the city band shell that receives series concert funding from The Junior League of Buffalo, Inc. The festival spans nearly two weeks and includes a variety of entertainment.

Utopia

22" x 30" Private Collection

"This natural terrain is a place for reflection and contemplation. The spirit encourages a meaningful conversation with oneself or friends. I feel the peaceful mood, smell the fragrances and listen to the sounds of bird inflections. I am uplifted with the crisp flickering tapestry of light and shadow. The bigness of space is Utopia!" M.M.M.

Olmsted Parks, Buffalo Park and Parkway System, was the vision of the great American landscape artist, Frederick Law Olmsted, and his partner Calvert Vaux. Part of Olmsted's vision was to connect six parks: Delaware—the focus of the initial design; Martin Luther King Jr., formerly Humboldt; Front; South—which was to be home to twenty-three hundred different species of trees and shrubs; Cazenovia; and Riverside. Although the parkway system was never fully realized, Buffalo is very fortunate to have six wonderful parks designed by Olmsted and any one of them can be considered Utopia.

Evening Glow

22" x 30"   Corporate Collection

"I respond with feeling and energy to the excitement of industrial subjects.
The evening light mood was exquisite and there is nothing so beautiful as light.
It is a celebration!"   MMM

At one point, Buffalo was the largest grain unloading and transfer facility in the world. The operation consisted of fifteen mills, stretching a length of about one-quarter mile. Of these fifteen mills, only six are in operation today. The birthplace of the grain elevator was Buffalo where, in 1842, through the ingenuity of Joseph Dart and Robert Dunbar, the world's first steam-powered elevator to transfer and store grain opened.

Sweet & Savory SIDES

Broadway Market

Buffalo's famous Broadway Market has been the home of high-quality ethnic foods for 108 years. As immigrants flocked to the east side of Buffalo in the late 1800s, they looked for the continuation of Old World customs in their new and unfamiliar environment. While they wanted to enter the main-stream of city life, they also sought to preserve their Eastern European traditions and heritage. The city-owned Broadway Market was established in 1888. ➤

Buttermilk Placek

4 cups flour

1 tablespoon baking powder

1 teaspoon baking soda

2 eggs

2 cups sugar

½ cup butter, softened

1 teaspoon vanilla extract

2 cups buttermilk

⅔ cup sugar

½ cup flour

3 tablespoons butter, softened

◆ Grease and flour 2 loaf pans.

◆ Sift 4 cups flour, baking powder and baking soda together.

◆ Beat the eggs in a mixer bowl until pale yellow. Add 2 cups sugar, ½ cup butter and vanilla.

◆ Beat until creamy, scraping the bowl occasionally. Add the dry ingredients and buttermilk ½ at a time, mixing well after each addition. Spoon into the prepared loaf pans.

◆ Combine ⅔ cup sugar, ½ cup flour and 3 tablespoons butter in a bowl, stirring with a fork until crumbly. Sprinkle over the top of the batter.

◆ Bake at 350 degrees for 45 minutes or until the loaves test done.

◆ Cool in the pans on a wire rack. Invert onto a hard surface. Cut into slices.

◆ Makes 2 loaves.

Peppercorn and Chive Corn Bread

¾ cup yellow cornmeal

¾ cup flour

1 tablespoon sugar

1½ teaspoons cream of tartar

¾ teaspoon baking soda

½ teaspoon coarsely ground pepper

½ teaspoon salt

1 cup light sour cream

¼ cup snipped fresh chives

3 tablespoons melted butter

2 tablespoons milk

1 egg, beaten

A mixture of 1 cup sour milk or buttermilk and 3 tablespoons butter may be substituted for 1 cup sour cream. Prepare sour milk by combining 1 cup milk with 1 tablespoon vinegar or 1 tablespoon lemon juice.

◆ Combine the cornmeal, flour, sugar, cream of tartar, baking soda, pepper and salt in a bowl and mix well. Make a well in the center of the ingredients.

◆ Whisk the sour cream, chives, butter, milk and egg together in a bowl. Spoon into the well of the dry ingredients, stirring just until blended. Spoon the batter into a buttered 8-inch square baking dish.

◆ Bake at 425 degrees for 20 minutes or until golden brown and the edges begin to pull from the sides of the dish. Cool slightly. Cut into squares.

◆ Makes 8 servings.

The Broadway Market quickly became a community meeting place, ideal for combining business with socializing and for sharing the latest in gossip and news from the Old World.

Today, nearly fifty independent merchants help to preserve the Eastern European heritage and traditions in businesses that include butcher shops, poultry stands, fruit/vegetable stands, bakeries, candy shops, delis, and restaurants.

Greek Olive and Tomato Focaccia

3½ teaspoons dry yeast

1 teaspoon sugar

1¾ cups lukewarm water

5½ cups flour

5 tablespoons olive oil

1 teaspoon salt

12 ounces Greek olives, pitted, chopped

5⅓ ounces Roma tomatoes, sliced

1½ tablespoons olive oil

1 teaspoon marjoram

½ teaspoon basil

Salt to taste

1½ tablespoons olive oil

2 cups crumbled feta cheese

◆ Combine the yeast, sugar and luke-warm water in a bowl and mix well.

◆ Let stand for 5 minutes or until foamy. Stir in the flour, 5 tablespoons olive oil and 1 teaspoon salt.

◆ Knead on a lightly floured surface for 3 minutes or until the dough is sticky. Place in a greased bowl, turning to coat the surface.

◆ Let rise, covered, in a warm place for 1½ hours. Punch the dough down. Pat into a greased 10x15-inch baking pan.

◆ Let rise for 1 hour.

◆ Combine the olives, tomatoes, 1½ tablespoons olive oil, marjoram, basil and salt to taste in a bowl and mix gently. Spread on a baking sheet.

◆ Bake at 450 degrees for 20 to 25 minutes or until the juices evaporate from the tomatoes, turning once. Remove from oven. Reduce the oven temperature to 400 degrees.

◆ Make indentations in the dough; drizzle with the remaining 1½ tablespoons olive oil. Sprinkle with the cheese. Top with the tomato mixture.

◆ Bake for 35 to 40 minutes; tent with foil if topping browns before dough.

◆ Makes 10 to 12 servings.

Marjoram is an aromatic herb belonging to the mint family. Sweet marjoram, the most common variety, has a mild, sweet oregano flavor.

More bagels are manufactured in Buffalo than in any other city in the country.

Irish Soda Bread

1 cup raisins

1 tablespoon rum or water

4 cups flour

⅔ cup sugar

1 teaspoon baking soda

1 teaspoon salt

¾ cup margarine, softened

1¼ cups buttermilk

1 tablespoon caraway seeds

◆ Combine the raisins and rum in a microwave-safe dish. Microwave on High for 30 seconds to plump.

◆ Combine the flour, sugar, baking soda and salt in a bowl. Cut in the margarine until crumbly. Stir in the buttermilk. Add raisins and caraway seeds, stirring just until mixed.

◆ Knead on a lightly floured surface about 20 times or until well mixed. Divide the dough into 2 equal portions. Shape each portion into a small round loaf. Place on an ungreased baking sheet.

◆ Bake at 350 degrees for 45 to 50 minutes or until the loaves test done. Serve warm with lots of butter.

◆ Makes 2 small loaves.

Pear Bread Extraordinaire

2 cups flour

½ teaspoon baking powder

⅛ teaspoon nutmeg

1 cup sugar

½ cup butter, softened

2 eggs

¼ cup yogurt or buttermilk

1 cup chopped pears

1 teaspoon vanilla extract

◆ Combine the flour, baking powder and nutmeg in a bowl and mix well.

◆ Beat the sugar and butter in a mixer bowl until creamy, scraping the bowl occasionally. Beat in the eggs 1 at a time. Add the dry ingredients and yogurt and mix well. Stir in the pears. Add the vanilla and mix well. Spoon into a buttered loaf pan.

◆ Bake at 350 degrees for 1 hour. Invert onto a wire rack.

◆ Let stand until cool. Cut into slices. Serve with cream cheese.

◆ Makes 1 loaf.

After being involved in an accident on Delaware Avenue in 1916, John Roffo Oishei invented the windshield wiper.

Deluxe Pineapple-Zucchini Bread

Frost this bread with your favorite cream cheese frosting or with a dusting of confectioners' sugar.

2 cups packed brown sugar

1 cup vegetable oil

1 cup shredded coconut

½ cup chopped walnuts

4 eggs, beaten

2 cups sifted flour

2 teaspoons cinnamon

1 teaspoon baking powder

1 teaspoon baking soda

1 teaspoon salt

1 (8-ounce) can crushed pineapple, well drained

2 cups shredded zucchini, well drained

2 teaspoons vanilla extract

◆ Combine the brown sugar, oil, coconut, walnuts and eggs in a bowl and mix well.

◆ Combine the flour, cinnamon, baking powder, baking soda and salt in a bowl and mix well. Add to brown sugar mixture.

◆ Beat for 2 minutes. Stir in the pineapple, zucchini and vanilla. Spoon into 2 loaf pans or 1 bundt pan sprayed with nonstick cooking spray.

◆ Bake at 350 degrees for 1 hour and 10 minutes or until the loaves test done.

◆ Makes 2 loaves or 1 bundt loaf.

Shredding refers to cutting or shaving ingredients into slivers.

St. Paul's Cathedral is Buffalo's oldest functioning church still located at its original site. It was given National Historic Landmark status in 1987 for its Gothic Revival architecture. St. Paul's was designed by Richard Upjohn, more famously known for his Trinity Church on Wall Street in New York City.

Oatmeal-Banana Muffins

¾ cup quick-cooking or rolled oats

½ cup milk

1 cup flour

½ cup sugar

2½ teaspoons baking powder

½ teaspoon baking soda

½ teaspoon salt

½ teaspoon cinnamon

¼ teaspoon nutmeg

1 cup mashed bananas

¼ cup melted butter or margarine

1 egg

◆ Combine the oats and milk in a bowl and mix well. Let stand until the milk is absorbed.

◆ Combine the flour, sugar, baking powder, baking soda, salt, cinnamon and nutmeg in a bowl and mix well.

◆ Combine the bananas, butter and egg in a bowl and mix well. Stir into the oat mixture. Add to the dry ingredients, mixing just until moistened; batter will be lumpy.

◆ Fill greased or paper-lined muffin cups ⅔ full.

◆ Bake at 425 degrees for 15 minutes or until the muffins test done. Remove to a wire rack to cool. May be frozen for future use; reheat before serving.

◆ Makes 12 to 14 muffins.

Carrot-Pineapple Muffins

1 cup sugar

⅔ cup vegetable oil

2 eggs

1 teaspoon vanilla extract

1½ cups sifted flour

1 teaspoon each baking powder and baking soda

½ teaspoon salt

¼ teaspoon cinnamon

1 cup grated carrots

½ cup crushed pineapple

◆ Combine the sugar, oil, eggs and vanilla in a bowl and mix well.

◆ Combine the flour, baking powder, baking soda, salt and cinnamon in a bowl and mix well. Add to the sugar mixture, stirring just until blended. Stir in the carrots and undrained pineapple gently.

◆ Fill 24 greased or paper-lined muffin cups ⅔ full.

◆ Bake at 325 degrees for 25 minutes or until the muffins test done.

◆ Makes 24 muffins.

General Mills manufactures Gold Medal Flour, Cheerios, Wheaties, Bisquick, and Betty Crocker mixes at their plant located in Buffalo.

Merk's Coffee Cake

This recipe has been passed around by family and friends for some years and rumor has it that 'Merk' is the woman from Ohio who originated it . . . this is an awesome coffee cake. Serve for a leisurely holiday or Sunday brunch with a fruit salad and a frittata.

2 cups sifted flour

1 teaspoon baking powder

1 teaspoon baking soda

¾ cup sugar

½ cup shortening

1 teaspoon vanilla extract

3 eggs

1 cup sour cream

1 cup packed brown sugar

6 tablespoons butter or
   margarine, softened

2 teaspoons cinnamon

1 cup chopped nuts

◆ Grease a 10-inch tube pan; line the bottom with waxed paper.

◆ Sift the flour, baking powder and baking soda together.

◆ Beat the sugar, shortening and vanilla in a mixer bowl until creamy, scraping the bowl occasionally. Add the eggs 1 at a time, beating well after each addition.

◆ Add the dry ingredients alternately with the sour cream, mixing after each addition. Spread ½ of the batter in the prepared tube pan.

◆ Beat the brown sugar, butter and cinnamon in a mixer bowl until creamy, scraping the bowl occasionally. Stir in the nuts. Dot ½ of the nut mixture over the prepared layer. Spread with the remaining batter. Dot with the remaining nut mixture.

◆ Bake at 350 degrees for 50 minutes or until the coffee cake tests done.

◆ Makes 16 servings.

Buffalo is the largest flour milling city in the world. At its peak, Buffalo milled 17,762,500 cwt. (hundredweight).

Buttermilk Pancakes and Devonshire Cream

This is a local family's tradition with "Breakfast at Wimbledon" and the advent of the Western New York strawberry season.

2 cups buttermilk

2 egg yolks

2 tablespoons melted
    margarine or
    vegetable oil

2 cups flour

2 tablespoons sugar

2 teaspoons baking soda

⅛ teaspoon salt

2 egg whites

Devonshire Cream (below)

◆ Combine the buttermilk, egg yolks and margarine in a bowl and mix well. Stir in a sifted mixture of the flour, sugar, baking soda and salt.

◆ Beat the egg whites in a mixer bowl until stiff. Fold into the buttermilk mixture.

◆ Grease a griddle or skillet lightly. Heat over medium heat until a few drops of cold water sprinkled on the surface sizzle. Pour ¼ cup batter at a time onto the hot griddle.

◆ Bake until brown on both sides, turning once. Spoon the Devonshire Cream over the pancakes.

◆ Makes 4 to 6 servings.

Devonshire Cream

½ cup sour cream

½ cup whipping cream

1 tablespoon sugar

1 to 2 cups sliced
    strawberries

Juice of 1 lemon or lime

◆ Combine the sour cream and whipping cream in a mixer bowl.

◆ Beat until soft peaks form, scraping the bowl occasionally. Add the sugar.

◆ Beat until firm, not stiff, peaks are formed. Fold in the strawberries and lemon juice.

◆ Makes 2 cups.

William M. Carrier of Evans, New York, was the first person to take the air conditioner and make it practical for general use.

Apple Orchard Pancakes

1½ cups rolled oats

1½ cups boiling water

1 cup unbleached flour

¼ cup sugar

2 tablespoons baking
  powder

1 egg

⅛ teaspoon salt

3 Northern Spy or Jona-
  Gold apples, peeled,
  chopped

½ to ¾ cup chopped pecans

1 cup milk

¼ cup melted butter

2 tablespoons butter

◆ Combine the oats and boiling water in a bowl and mix well.

◆ Let stand for 5 minutes. Add the flour, sugar, baking powder, egg and salt and mix gently. Stir in the apples, pecans, milk and ¼ cup melted butter.

◆ Heat 2 tablespoons butter on a griddle or in a skillet until sizzling. Pour ¼ cup of the batter at a time onto the hot griddle.

◆ Bake for 3 to 5 minutes or until bubbles appear on the surface and the underside is brown. Turn the pancake over.

◆ Bake for 2 to 3 minutes longer or until golden brown. Serve with maple syrup.

◆ Makes 4 servings.

Cinnamon Whole Wheat Pancakes

½ cup sifted all-purpose
  flour

2 teaspoons cinnamon

¾ teaspoon baking soda

½ teaspoon baking powder

½ teaspoon salt

½ teaspoon nutmeg

1 cup whole wheat flour

2 cups buttermilk

3 tablespoons sugar

2 tablespoons melted butter

1 egg

◆ Sift the flour, cinnamon, baking soda, baking powder, salt and nutmeg into a bowl and mix well. Stir in the whole wheat flour.

◆ Combine the buttermilk, sugar, butter and egg in a bowl and mix well. Add to the flour mixture, mixing just until moistened.

◆ Heat a lightly greased griddle to 350 degrees. Pour ¼ cup of the batter at a time onto the hot griddle.

◆ Bake until brown on both sides, turning once.

◆ Makes 4 servings.

New York is the second-largest producer of maple syrup.

Shea's Buffalo Center for the Performing Arts

Shea's Buffalo was constructed in 1926 and named after Michael Shea, the most prominent theater owner and operator in Buffalo's history. The theater is considered one of the best motion picture palaces of the 1920s. The interior was baroque with murals and ceiling decorations. In its time, Shea's locally opened all the great films of vintage stars.

In 1974, the theater underwent a major restoration. Currently, the theater is used for traveling music shows, dance companies, rock groups, and opera.

Asparagus with Wine Sauce

1 pound fresh asparagus, trimmed or 2 (10-ounce) packages frozen asparagus

¾ cup mushrooms

2 tablespoons butter

2 tablespoons flour

½ teaspoon salt

⅛ teaspoon pepper

1 cup half-and-half

½ cup dry white wine

½ cup shredded Cheddar cheese

½ cup almonds

When preparing fresh asparagus, break the stalks . . . they will snap where the tender part starts.

◆ Arrange the asparagus in a baking pan.

◆ Sauté the mushrooms in the butter in a saucepan. Stir in the flour, salt and pepper. Add the half-and-half and wine and mix well.

◆ Cook over medium heat until thickened, stirring constantly. Pour over the asparagus. Sprinkle with the cheese and almonds.

◆ Bake at 450 degrees for 15 minutes or until the cheese melts.

◆ Makes 6 servings.

Ol' Settlers' Baked Beans

Great for picnics with hot dogs and hamburgers.

8 ounces ground sirloin

8 ounces bacon, chopped

1 onion, chopped

1 (16-ounce) can kidney beans

1 (16-ounce) can lima beans, drained

1 (16-ounce) can pork and beans

½ cup packed brown sugar

⅓ cup sugar

¼ cup catsup

¼ cup barbecue sauce

2 tablespoons prepared mustard

2 tablespoons molasses

1 teaspoon chili powder

1 teaspoon salt

¼ teaspoon pepper

◆ Brown the ground sirloin, bacon and onion in a large skillet, stirring frequently; drain. Stir in the kidney beans, lima beans, pork and beans, brown sugar, sugar, catsup, barbecue sauce, prepared mustard, molasses, chili powder, salt and pepper. Spoon into a 9x13-inch baking pan.

◆ Two tablespoons honey or corn syrup may be substituted for the molasses and 2 teaspoons dry mustard for the prepared mustard.

◆ Bake, uncovered, at 350 degrees for 1 hour.

◆ Makes 8 to 12 servings.

The *"Thomas Flyer"* racing car, which won the Great Auto Race from New York to Paris, France, was built at the Pierce Arrow Company and was driven by George Schuster of Springville.

Cheese-Crusted Barbecued Beans

2 medium Vidalia onions,
  coarsely chopped

1 clove of garlic, minced

2 tablespoons vegetable oil

4 (16-ounce) cans plain
  baked beans, drained

½ cup catsup

¼ cup light molasses

1 cup shredded sharp
  Cheddar cheese

½ cup dry bread crumbs

2 tablespoons melted butter
  or margarine

◆ Sauté the onions and garlic in the oil
  in a saucepan for 5 minutes or until
  golden brown and tender. Remove
  from heat.

◆ Stir in the beans, catsup and molasses.
  Spoon into a 2-quart baking dish.

◆ Combine the cheese, bread crumbs
  and butter in a bowl and mix well.
  Sprinkle over the bean mixture.

◆ Bake at 350 degrees for 30 minutes or
  until brown and bubbly.

◆ Makes 12 to 16 servings.

Sweet onions, such as
Vidalia, are usually only
available seasonally. More
robust onions can be
sweetened by soaking in
milk for several minutes
after slicing or chopping.

The Grand Athenaeum
Hotel on the grounds of
Chautauqua Institute
was one of the first
buildings anywhere to
have electricity.

Brussels Sprouts Moutarde

*2 pints fresh brussels
  sprouts, trimmed*

Salt to taste

½ cup chopped onion

2 tablespoons butter

1 tablespoon flour

1 tablespoon brown sugar

1 teaspoon salt

½ teaspoon dry mustard

½ cup milk

1 cup sour cream

*1 tablespoon snipped fresh
  parsley*

◆ Cut any large brussels sprouts into halves. Combine the brussels sprouts and salt with just enough water to cover in a saucepan.

◆ Cook, covered, for 10 to 15 minutes or until of the desired degree of crispness; drain.

◆ Sauté the onion in the butter in a saucepan until tender but not brown. Stir in the flour, brown sugar, salt and dry mustard. Add the milk and mix well.

◆ Cook until thickened, stirring constantly. Blend in the sour cream. Stir in the brussels sprouts.

◆ Cook just until heated through, stirring frequently; do not boil. Spoon into a serving bowl; sprinkle with the parsley.

◆ Makes 2 to 3 servings.

*To protest the
dehumanization of man
during the Industrial
Revolution, Elbert
Hubbard established the
Roycroft Arts and
Crafts Colony in East
Aurora circa 1894.*

Youngstown/ Lewiston

When visiting the Youngstown/Lewiston area, one can not only become overwhelmed by the history in the area, but also by the beautiful surroundings. You can take a walk through Fort Niagara, which was the scene of many wars dating back to 1726 when the Fort was built. Another favorite spot in the area is Artpark. It not only shows off the ➤

Corn Fritters with Orange Sauce

1 (10-ounce) package
   frozen whole kernel
   corn, thawed

Milk

½ cup flour

2 tablespoons melted butter
   or margarine

1 teaspoon salt

¾ teaspoon baking powder

⅛ teaspoon pepper

2 eggs, beaten

Vegetable oil for frying

Orange Sauce (below)

◆ Drain the corn, reserving the liquid.

◆ Combine the reserved liquid with enough milk to measure ¼ cup.

◆ Combine the milk mixture, corn, flour, butter, salt, baking powder, pepper and eggs in a bowl and mix well.

◆ Pour the oil into a skillet to a depth of ½ inch. Heat until oil is hot.

◆ Drop the batter by tablespoonfuls into the hot oil.

◆ Fry until golden brown on both sides; drain.

◆ Drizzle the Orange Sauce over the corn fritters.

◆ Makes 4 to 6 servings.

Orange Sauce

1 cup sweet orange
   marmalade

¼ cup butter or margarine

◆ Combine the marmalade and butter in a saucepan.

◆ Cook until mixed and heated through, stirring constantly.

◆ Makes 4 to 6 servings.

Italian Baked Eggplant

1 large eggplant

1 clove of garlic, thinly
  sliced

¼ cup olive oil

1 large white onion, finely
  chopped

1 rib celery, peeled, finely
  chopped

1 (15-ounce) can stewed
  tomatoes

1 tablespoon sugar

1 teaspoon finely chopped
  fresh basil

Salt and pepper to taste

½ cup shredded sharp
  Cheddar cheese

◆ Cut the eggplant lengthwise into
  halves. Scoop out the pulp carefully,
  leaving the shells intact. Chop the pulp
  into ½-inch pieces.

◆ Sauté the garlic in the olive oil in a
  12-inch skillet for 2 minutes. Add the
  eggplant pulp, onion and celery;
  reduce heat to medium.

◆ Sauté for 10 minutes or until the
  vegetables are tender, stirring
  frequently. Stir in the undrained
  tomatoes.

◆ Cook until thickened and most of
  the liquid has evaporated, stirring
  frequently. Add the sugar, basil, salt
  and pepper and mix well. Spoon into
  the shells; sprinkle with the cheese.

◆ Arrange the stuffed shells in a shallow
  baking dish; pour hot water to a depth
  of ½ inch around the shells.

◆ Bake at 375 degrees for 20 to 30
  minutes or until light brown.

◆ Makes 2 servings.

Niagara Gorge, but
more importantly shows
off local artists and
craftsmen, as well as
hosts many different
productions in the theaters.
Another point of interest
and a significant
archeological find is the
Lewiston Mound, which
dates back more than four
thousand years to the
Hopewell Indians and is
located near the Lewiston
Portage Landing Site.

The Genesee Country Museum has a unique horticulture collection, including an heirloom vegetable garden.

Stuffed Escarole Casserole

This tastes like a gourmet stuffed artichoke. Great with pork or lamb.

1 large head escarole

1 cup plain bread crumbs

1 cup seasoned bread crumbs

1 cup (heaping) grated Romano cheese

2 teaspoons garlic powder

⅓ cup olive oil

◆ Place the entire head of escarole in a 2-quart baking dish; open the leaves.

◆ Combine the bread crumbs, cheese and garlic powder in a bowl and mix well. Sprinkle over the leaves. Drizzle with the olive oil. Press the leaves down into the baking dish.

◆ Bake, covered, at 350 degrees for 25 minutes.

◆ Makes 6 servings.

Potatoes Foster

2½ pounds potatoes, peeled

2 medium onions, chopped

6 tablespoons butter

3 cups shredded Cheddar cheese

2 cups sour cream

◆ Combine the potatoes with enough water to cover in a saucepan. Bring to a boil.

◆ Boil for 45 minutes or until tender; drain. Mash the potatoes. Sauté the onions in the butter in a skillet for 3 minutes or until tender. Stir in the cheese and sour cream.

◆ Cook until the cheese melts, stirring constantly. Add the potatoes, tossing to mix. Spoon into a greased baking pan.

◆ Bake at 350 degrees for 45 to 60 minutes or until the top is crusty and brown.

◆ Makes 6 servings.

Roasted Garlic Mashed Potatoes

1 head garlic

1 tablespoon olive oil

1 bunch green onions,
    chopped

2 tablespoons butter or
    margarine

6 large red potatoes, cut
    into ¼-inch pieces

6 ounces regular or low-fat
    cream cheese, softened,
    cubed

Freshly ground pepper

Paprika

———◆———

*Fit a pastry bag with a
large star-shaped tip. Flute
the potato mixture into
individual cones in a
baking pan sprayed with
nonstick cooking spray
and lightly sprinkled with
paprika. Bake at 300
degrees for 10 minutes.*

◆ Cut ⅛ to ¼ inch from the top of
   the garlic head to expose the cloves.
   Place in a baking pan. Drizzle with
   the olive oil.

◆ Bake at 350 degrees for 45 to 60
   minutes or until brown. Remove from
   oven. Pop cloves out of skin and mash
   when cool.

◆ Sauté the green onions in the butter in
   a skillet just until tender.

◆ Combine the potatoes with enough
   water to cover in a saucepan. Bring to
   a boil; reduce heat.

◆ Cook, covered, for 10 minutes or until
   tender; drain. Mash the potatoes. Stir in
   the garlic, green onions, cream cheese
   and pepper. Spoon into a baking dish
   sprinkled with paprika.

◆ May be prepared 1 day in advance
   and stored in the refrigerator. Bring the
   mashed potatoes to room temperature
   before reheating. May roast the garlic
   1 day in advance or while cooking the
   potatoes.

◆ Bake at 300 degrees for 10 minutes or
   until light brown.

◆ Makes 6 servings.

M.J.'s Stuffed Pumpkins

4 small cooking pumpkins
  with stems

2 loaves dry Italian bread

3 cups julienned carrots

2 cups julienned zucchini

2 cups julienned yellow
  squash

1 onion, chopped

1 eggplant, chopped

2 ripe tomatoes, chopped

10 mushrooms, sliced

3 cloves of garlic, chopped

1 tablespoon olive oil

2 cups vegetable stock

½ teaspoon salt

½ teaspoon pepper

½ teaspoon nutmeg

Juice of 1 lemon

4 cups water

◆ Cut a circle around the stem of each pumpkin. Remove and reserve the circles to use as garnishes. Discard the seeds from the pumpkin shells.

◆ Remove the center of each bread loaf, leaving the crust; discard the crust. Crumble the bread into a bowl.

◆ Sauté the carrots, zucchini, yellow squash, onion, eggplant, tomatoes, mushrooms and garlic in the olive oil in a skillet until tender. Add the sautéed vegetables and vegetable stock to the bread and mix well. Stir in the salt, pepper and nutmeg. Spoon into the pumpkins; drizzle with the lemon juice.

◆ Arrange the pumpkins in a 9x13-inch baking dish. Pour the water around the pumpkins.

◆ Bake, covered with foil, at 350 degrees for 25 to 40 minutes or until done to taste.

◆ Remove the pumpkins to a serving platter. Attach a pumpkin circle with stem to the side of each pumpkin for garnish.

◆ Makes 4 servings.

Roasted Root Vegetables

A healthy winter side dish that is great served with beef or pork roast.

8 carrots, cut into 2-inch
    slices

6 parsnips, cut into quarters

6 turnips, cut into quarters

6 leek bulbs, cut into
    quarters

6 red potatoes, cut into
    quarters

4 kohlrabi, cut into quarters

2 red onions, cut into 1½-
    inch pieces

1 head garlic, separated
    into cloves

6 tablespoons vegetable oil
    or olive oil

2 cups chicken stock

1 envelope onion soup mix

Salt and pepper to taste

◆ Sauté the carrots, parsnips, turnips, leeks, red potatoes, kohlrabi, onions and garlic in batches in the oil in a skillet until light brown; use 1 to 2 tablespoons of oil per batch.

◆ May sauté the vegetables in advance and store in the refrigerator. Bring to room temperature before roasting.

◆ Spoon the sautéed vegetables into a roasting pan. Stir in the stock and soup mix.

◆ Roast at 350 degrees for 1 to 1½ hours or until done to taste, adding additional stock as needed. Season with salt and pepper.

◆ Makes 6 to 10 servings.

Prevent teary eyes by quartering the onions under cold running water.

Buffalo receives only 8.69 inches of precipitation from June through August, making it one of the driest cities in the Northeast.

Cheese Spinach Bake

2 (10-ounce) packages
    frozen chopped spinach

1½ cups small curd cottage
    cheese

4 ounces Cheddar cheese,
    shredded

¼ cup butter, softened

3 eggs, beaten

2 teaspoons flour

Salt and pepper to taste

◆ Cook the spinach using package
   directions; drain.

◆ Combine the spinach, cottage cheese,
   Cheddar cheese, butter, eggs, flour,
   salt and pepper in a bowl and mix
   well. Spoon into a greased 1-quart
   baking dish.

◆ Bake at 350 degrees for 1 hour.

◆ Makes 4 servings.

Coconutty Sweet Potatoes

3 (16-ounce) cans sweet
    potatoes, drained

½ cup sugar

¼ cup milk

2 tablespoons butter

2 eggs

½ teaspoon vanilla extract

½ cup shredded coconut

½ cup chopped pecans

½ cup packed brown sugar

3 tablespoons flour

3 tablespoons melted butter

◆ Combine the sweet potatoes, sugar,
   milk, 2 tablespoons butter, eggs and
   vanilla in a bowl. Mash until blended.
   Spoon into a 9x13-inch baking dish.

◆ Combine the coconut, pecans, brown
   sugar and flour in a bowl and mix
   well. Stir in 3 tablespoons melted
   butter. Spread over the sweet potatoes.

◆ Bake at 375 degrees for 30 to 40
   minutes or until light brown and
   bubbly.

◆ Makes 8 servings.

*At the turn of the
century, Buffalo had
more millionaires than
any other city in
the country.*

Spinach Risotto

4 cups chicken broth

6 shallots, or 1 small onion, chopped

1 tablespoon chopped garlic

1 tablespoon olive oil

1 cup arborio rice

1 cup undrained thawed frozen spinach

2 tablespoons basil pesto

1 teaspoon thyme

Salt and pepper to taste

½ cup grated Parmesan cheese

———◆———

Arborio rice is the essential ingredient in risotto which is a classic Northern Italian rice dish. The grains will swell to two or three times their original size. They will be plump and round and have a moist, creamy consistency but slightly firm when cooked. The secret to a perfect risotto is to cook it very slowly over low heat until all the liquid has been absorbed.

◆ Bring the broth just to a boil in a heavy saucepan; reduce heat to simmer. Simmer while preparing risotto.

◆ Sauté the shallots and garlic in the olive oil in a sauté pan for 5 minutes or until tender. Stir in the rice.

◆ Sauté for 3 minutes, stirring constantly. Stir in 1 cup of the broth.

◆ Cook until the broth is absorbed, stirring constantly. Add ½ cup of the broth and mix well.

◆ Cook until almost absorbed, stirring constantly. Stir in the spinach, basil pesto and thyme. Add the remaining 2½ cups broth ½ cup at a time.

◆ Cook until the broth is absorbed between each addition, stirring constantly. Test the consistency of the rice before adding the entire amount of the broth. The mixture should be creamy but each grain should be separate and firm. Season with salt and pepper. Stir in the cheese. Serve immediately.

◆ Makes 4 to 6 servings.

Albright-Knox Art Gallery

The Albright-Knox Art Gallery enjoys a worldwide reputation as an outstanding center of modern art. Its collection has been cited as "one of the world's top international surveys of contemporary painting and sculpture" and is especially rich in American and European art of the past fifty years, mostly acquired through the farsighted generosity of its patron, the late ➤

Confetti Rice

Try substituting dried cherries or cranberries for raisins and/or pecans, walnuts, or almonds for pine nuts.

1 cup raisins

¾ cup long grain white rice

¾ cup brown rice

½ cup wild rice

1½ cups chicken stock

6 tablespoons unsalted butter

6 tablespoons chopped onion

2¾ cups chicken stock

½ cup shredded carrot

3 tablespoons unsalted butter

1 cup pine nuts, toasted

½ cup chopped fresh parsley

———◆———

A large carrot will yield one cup of shredded carrot.

◆ Plump the raisins in enough hot water to cover in a bowl; drain.

◆ Rinse the white rice, brown rice and wild rice separately and drain.

◆ Combine the wild rice and 1½ cups stock in a saucepan and mix well.

◆ Cook, covered, for 35 to 40 minutes or until tender.

◆ Heat 3 tablespoons of butter in each of 2 separate saucepans until melted. Add 3 tablespoons chopped onion to each saucepan. Sauté until tender.

◆ Add the white rice and 1¼ cups of the chicken stock to 1 saucepan and mix well. Add the brown rice and the remaining 1½ cups stock to the remaining saucepan and mix well.

◆ Bring both saucepans to a boil; reduce heat to simmer. Simmer the white rice, covered, for 20 minutes and the brown rice, covered, for 1 hour.

◆ Sauté the carrot in 3 tablespoons butter in a skillet.

◆ Combine the white rice, brown rice and wild rice in a bowl and mix well. Stir in the raisins, carrot, pine nuts and parsley. Spoon into a serving bowl.

◆ Makes 8 servings.

Hot Jamaican Rice

1 medium onion, chopped

2 cloves of garlic, crushed

¼ cup butter

2 cups chicken stock

1 cup coconut milk

Jamaican hot sauce to taste

1½ cups uncooked rice

1 (8-ounce) can kidney
   beans or pinto beans

◆ Sauté the onion and garlic in the butter
   in a saucepan until tender. Stir in the
   stock, coconut milk and hot sauce.
   Add the rice and mix well. Bring to a
   boil; reduce heat.

◆ Cook, covered, for 10 minutes. Add the
   beans and mix well.

◆ Cook for 10 minutes longer or until all
   the liquid is absorbed and the rice is
   tender.

◆ Makes 2 to 4 servings.

Putting-on-the-Ritz Pineapple

Serve with a roast or ham.

1 sleeve Ritz crackers,
   crumbled

3 tablespoons melted butter

4 ounces white sharp
   Cheddar cheese,
   shredded

⅓ cup sugar

2 tablespoons flour

1 (16-ounce) can crushed
   pineapple, drained

1 (16-ounce) can pineapple
   chunks, drained

◆ Combine the crackers and butter in a
   bowl, tossing to mix. Spread on a
   baking sheet.

◆ Toast at 325 degrees until golden
   brown.

◆ Combine the cheese, sugar and flour
   in a bowl and mix well. Stir in the
   crushed pineapple and pineapple
   chunks. Spoon into a baking dish.
   Sprinkle with the cracker mixture.

◆ Bake at 350 degrees for 30 minutes.

◆ Makes 8 to 10 servings.

Seymour H. Knox. The
Gallery's magnificent
main building, designed
in the Greek Revival
style by Edward
B. Green in 1904, was
made possible through
the munificence of John
J. Albright. The new
addition, designed by
Gordon Bunshaft of
Skidmore, Owings, and
Merrill, and donated by
Seymour H. Knox, his
family, and others, was
inaugurated in 1962.

Sausage and Tomato Polenta

*Polenta may be served as a side dish with a meat entrée
or with a salad as a light meal.*

2 hot Italian sausages

1 small onion, chopped

1 tablespoon olive oil

4 plum tomatoes

1½ cups milk

½ teaspoon flour

½ teaspoon sugar

¼ teaspoon salt

½ cup yellow cornmeal

¼ cup grated Parmesan
cheese

———————◆———————

*Polenta became popular
in the Lombardi Venteo
region around Venice.
This yellow maize flour
(cornmeal) is boiled and
then served steaming hot
with stews. The polenta may
be cooled, cut into slices,
and then broiled, baked, or
fried in olive oil. Preparing
polenta is time-consuming
because it needs continuous
stirring to achieve a smooth
lump-free finish. Quick
polenta is available in most
grocery stores.*

◆ Remove sausage casings and crumble sausage.

◆ Sauté the onion in the olive oil in a heavy saucepan until tender. Add the sausage.

◆ Cook for 10 minutes or until the sausage is brown, stirring constantly. Add the plum tomatoes.

◆ Cook for 2 minutes, stirring frequently. Stir in the milk, flour, sugar and salt.

◆ Cook until heated through; reduce heat to simmer.

◆ Add the cornmeal in a fine stream, whisking constantly until mixed.

◆ Simmer for 10 minutes or until the mixture has thickened and the edge pulls from the side of the saucepan, stirring constantly with a wooden spoon. Stir in the cheese. Remove from heat immediately.

◆ Spoon into individual bowls.

◆ The polenta will become firm after cooling. Leftovers may be sliced and reheated in a greased skillet.

◆ Makes 4 servings.

Pineapple Salsa

1 fresh pineapple, chopped

1 medium red onion, chopped

3 tablespoons chopped seeded jalapeños

◆ Combine the pineapple, onion and jalapeños in a bowl and mix well.

◆ Chill, covered, for 2 hours.

◆ Serve with tortilla chips or as an accompaniment to grilled fish or chicken.

◆ Makes 3 to 4 cups.

Festive Peach Salsa

2½ cups chopped peeled peaches

⅓ cup chopped sweet onion

3½ tablespoons lime juice

2 to 3 tablespoons finely chopped seeded jalapeños

1 or 2 cloves of garlic, minced

1 to 2 tablespoons chopped fresh cilantro

¾ teaspoon sugar

◆ Combine the peaches, onion, lime juice, jalapeños, garlic, cilantro and sugar in a bowl and mix gently.

◆ Chill, covered, for 1 to 2 hours.

◆ Serve as an accompaniment to chicken, fish, Mexican dishes or pork, or as a dip with tortilla chips or pita triangles.

◆ Makes 3 cups.

Prepare pita triangles by splitting pitas into single rounds. Spray each round with nonstick olive oil cooking spray or brush lightly with olive oil. Cut each round into wedges. Bake at 350 degrees for 8 minutes. Sprinkle with salt, rosemary, cayenne, or dillweed.

Herbert Hauptmann, president of the Medical Foundation of Buffalo, gained international fame in 1985 for winning the Nobel Prize.

Louise Blanchard, the nation's first female architect, was one of the planners of Buffalo's Lafayette Hotel.

Garden Chili

3 cloves of garlic, finely chopped

1 tablespoon olive oil

1 (28-ounce) can Italian-style tomatoes

1 (6-ounce) can tomato paste

1 (16-ounce) can Northern beans

1 (16-ounce) can black beans

1 (16-ounce) can kidney beans

1 tablespoon chili powder

1 tablespoon basil

1 tablespoon oregano

1 teaspoon black pepper

⅛ teaspoon cayenne (optional)

1 cup chopped carrots

1 medium zucchini, shredded, or 1 cup shredded zucchini

1 cup whole kernel corn

◆ Sauté the garlic in the olive oil in a large saucepan. Stir in the undrained tomatoes, tomato paste, undrained beans, chili powder, basil, oregano, black pepper and cayenne. Bring to a boil; reduce heat.

◆ Simmer, covered, for 10 minutes, stirring occasionally. Stir in the carrots, zucchini and corn.

◆ Simmer for 30 minutes longer or until of the desired consistency, stirring occasionally. The flavor is enhanced the longer the cooking time. Ladle into chili bowls.

◆ Makes 6 to 8 servings.

Cold Green Tomato Soup with Black Truffle

10 artichoke hearts,
    chopped

4 leeks, chopped

2 shallots, minced

2 green bell peppers,
    chopped

2 ribs celery, chopped

5 tablespoons olive oil

5 pounds green tomatoes,
    chopped

2 quarts chicken stock

¼ cup Champagne vinegar

Salt and freshly ground
    white pepper to taste

1 small black truffle,
    minced

◆ Sauté the artichokes, leeks, shallots, green peppers and celery in the olive oil in a saucepan until tender; do not brown. Stir in the green tomatoes.

◆ Cook for 10 minutes or until the tomatoes begin to fall apart, stirring occasionally. Add the chicken stock and mix well. Bring to a boil; reduce heat.

◆ Simmer for 1 hour, stirring occasionally. Remove from heat.

◆ Let stand until cool. Chill, covered, in the refrigerator.

◆ Process in a food processor or blender until puréed.

◆ Combine the purée and Champagne vinegar in a bowl and mix well. Season with salt and white pepper. Stir in the truffle.

◆ Chill, covered, until serving time. Ladle into soup bowls.

◆ May substitute ¼ cup black truffle oil for the minced black truffle.

◆ Makes 8 to 10 servings.

The idea of high school was conceived by Sullivan Crane of Lockport, New York, in 1850. This concept was the first of its kind in the world.

Cold Vichyssoise or Hot Potato and Leek Soup

Serve hot or cold in the summer or winter.

2/3 to 3/4 cup chopped onion

1/4 cup butter or margarine

Seasoned salt to taste

1 1/2 pounds baking potatoes, peeled, chopped

4 cups chicken stock

1/4 cup butter or margarine

3 tablespoons flour

2 cups half-and-half or whipping cream

3/4 cup leek

2 teaspoons sugar

———◆———

May substitute 3/4 cup milk and 1/3 cup butter for 1 cup whipping cream.

◆ Cook the onion in 1/4 cup butter in a saucepan over low heat for 8 to 10 minutes or until tender, stirring frequently. Stir in the seasoned salt. Add the potatoes, and mix well.

◆ Cook until the potatoes are tender, stirring frequently. Stir in the chicken stock. Bring to a boil.

◆ Boil for 5 to 8 minutes, stirring occasionally. Adjust the seasonings.

◆ Heat 1/4 cup butter in a saucepan until melted. Add the flour and mix well. Stir into the potato mixture. Add the half-and-half and mix well. Stir in the leek and sugar. Add additional half-and-half or water for a thinner consistency; add additional flour and butter for a thicker consistency.

◆ Ladle into soup bowls.

◆ Makes 6 to 8 servings.

Father Demske's Mushroom Soup

2 tablespoons chicken
  bouillon granules

3 cups hot water

1 large onion, chopped

¼ cup butter

1 pound mushrooms,
  trimmed, sliced

⅓ cup minced fresh parsley

3 tablespoons tomato paste

1 clove of garlic, crushed

¼ teaspoon ground pepper

½ cup dry white wine

½ cup shredded Jarlsberg
  cheese

½ cup shredded asiago
  cheese

½ cup shredded sharp
  Cheddar cheese

◆ Dissolve the bouillon granules in the hot water and mix well.

◆ Sauté the onion in the butter in a stockpot over medium heat just until tender. Stir in the mushrooms.

◆ Sauté briefly. Add the bouillon mixture, parsley, tomato paste, garlic and pepper and mix well. May prepare in advance to this point and store in the refrigerator until just before serving.

◆ Stir in the white wine. Simmer, covered, for 5 minutes, stirring occasionally.

◆ Ladle into soup bowls. Sprinkle with the Jarlsberg cheese, asiago cheese and Cheddar cheese. Serve immediately.

◆ Makes 8 servings.

Ed Gibson, a graduate of Kenmore West Senior High School, distinguished himself as an astronaut serving aboard the *Skylab* from November 16, 1973, to February 8, 1974.

Red Pepper Chowder

A beautiful red color and a sweet peppery taste.

4 red bell peppers, chopped

2 leek bulbs, chopped

1 large carrot, cut into
matchstick strips

1 large onion, chopped

1 tablespoon butter

3 cups chicken broth

1½ cups whipping cream

Freshly ground pepper
to taste

◆ Sauté the red peppers, leeks, carrot and onion in the butter in a saucepan for 10 to 15 minutes or until tender. Reserve 1 cup of the vegetables.

◆ Process the remaining vegetables and 1 cup of the broth in a food processor until puréed. Return the purée and reserved vegetables to the saucepan. Stir in the remaining 2 cups of broth and whipping cream.

◆ Simmer until reduced by ⅓, stirring frequently. Remove from heat. Season with pepper.

◆ Ladle into soup bowls. Serve immediately.

◆ Makes 4 to 6 servings.

Eclectic
ENTRÉES

The Wilcox Mansion
22" x 30"

"A quick shower, the sun bursts forth . . . theatrics and beauty of light. A sudden, sparkling moment in time. One needs to take time to see." MMM

The Theodore Roosevelt Inaugural Site was erected in 1838 as a barracks during the Patriots' War in Canada. The American government ordered the barracks to be built when it feared war would break out. On September 14, 1901, Theodore Roosevelt took the oath of office as the twenty-sixth President of the United States in the library of the Wilcox Mansion, after President McKinley was assassinated during the Pan-American Exposition. In 1969, a Junior League of Buffalo donation was made to the Theodore Roosevelt Inaugural Site Foundation to spearhead a drive to restore the Wilcox Mansion.

Historical Museum

15" x 22"

"How wonderful it is when that moment of true seeing comes and I'm transported to that point when eyes, hand, mind and spirit come together. I cherish this fleeting moment when truth occurs—the never ending process of discovery." MMM

The Buffalo and Erie County Historical Society Building was constructed in 1901 as the New York State pavilion for the Pan-American Exposition. It is the only remaining structure of the Exposition. The "Street of 1870" exhibit, funded by the Junior League of Buffalo, reflects on the toils of the bakers, blacksmiths, weavers, and tailors from the days of yesteryear.

"I saw this subject as a stage setting. Shapes were seen before actual images. Contrasting light and shadow along with areas of rest and activity were used to draw attention to the monument focus and to direct the eye into the painting space. People add life as well as spacial dimension." MMM

Buffalo City Hall is truly an intermingling of the many different cultures in Buffalo. When standing in front of City Hall, above the eight columns of the main entrance the observer will find twenty-one figures carved, representing the various aspects of the city's cultural and economic life. Upon entering the building, one passes through bronze doors that bear the symbols of the Indian tribes who once inhabited the region. Once inside, the marble floors, mosaic ceilings, sculptured piers, and colorful murals are simply spectacular. Directly across from Buffalo's City Hall is the McKinley Monument. The McKinley Monument was erected in honor of President William McKinley, who was assassinated in Buffalo while attending the Pan-American Exposition. At the base of the monument there is a fountain supported by four lions symbolizing courage and strength, and four turtles representing eternity.

Eclectic ENTREES

Beef Tenderloin en
   Croûte, 78
Pot Roast with Roasted Root
   Vegetables, 79
Steak Shaniqua, 80
Veal with Three
   Mustards, 81
Veal in Wine Sauce with
   Spätzle, 82
Veal Shanks with Capers, 84
Pork Medallions au
   Poivre, 85
Currant Mustard Pork
   Tenderloin, 86
Herb-Crusted Lamb and
   Potatoes, 87
Grilled Lamb Chops with
   Gorgonzola Butter, 88
Greek Marinated
   Kabobs, 89
Herb-Marinated Lamb, 90
Chinese Fried Chicken
   Wings, 90
Buffalo Chicken Wings, 91
Bleu Cheese Dressing, 91
Curry-Glazed Sesame
   Wings, 92
Gingered Chicken Wings, 93

Almond-Orange
   Chicken, 94
Chicken with Balsamic
   Vinegar and
   Mushrooms, 95
Chicken Breasts with
   Mustard Seed Sauce, 96
Fruit-Glazed Chicken, 97
Grilled Bourbon
   Chicken, 97
Chicken Piccata, 98
Sunday Chicken, 99
Sherry Chicken for a
   Crowd, 100
Italian Sausage-Stuffed
   Squash, 101
Barbecued Duck Breasts
   on Sweet Corn
   Pancakes, 102
Crab Cakes, 104
Seafood Sauce, 105
Lobster Ginger, 106
Coquilles St. Jacques, 107
Crab-Stuffed Shrimp, 108
Shrimp Laurine, 109
Fillets of Sole Sauté, 110
Sesame Balsamic
   Tuna, 111

Thai Peanut Shrimp and
   Linguini, 112
Rigatoni with Chicken
   Fennel Mousse, 113
Rotini with Chicken,
   Gorgonzola Cheese
   and Peas, 114
Passion Pasta, 115
Angel Hair Pasta with
   Shrimp, Asparagus
   and Fresh Basil, 116
Jambalaya Pasta, 117
Seafood Pasta with
   Peppers and Greek
   Olives, 118
Chinese Pasta, 119
Penne with Bacon and
   Three Cheeses, 120
Penne with Mushrooms,
   Tomatoes and
   Gorgonzola Cheese, 121
Linguini with Roasted
   Yellow Pepper
   Sauce, 122
Pasta with Vodka, 123
Greek-Style Pasta and
   Phyllo, 124
Ultimate Pesto, 124

Beef Tenderloin en Croûte

1 (3- to 4-pound) beef
  tenderloin

12 ounces fresh mushrooms,
  finely chopped

2 tablespoons margarine

8 ounces herb cream cheese,
  softened

¼ cup seasoned bread
  crumbs

2 tablespoons madeira

1 tablespoon chopped fresh
  chives

¼ teaspoon salt

1 (17-ounce) package
  frozen puff pastry,
  thawed

1 egg, beaten

1 tablespoon cold water

———————◆———————

If the tenderloin is in two pieces, overlap the thinner ends and tie with kitchen twine at one-inch intervals.

◆ Place the tenderloin on a rack in a baking pan.

◆ Bake at 425 degrees for 45 to 50 minutes or until a meat thermometer registers 135 degrees. Cool in the refrigerator for 30 minutes.

◆ Sauté the mushrooms in the margarine in a skillet for 10 minutes or until the liquid evaporates, stirring occasionally. Stir in the cream cheese, bread crumbs, wine, chives and salt. Let stand until cool.

◆ Overlap the pastry sheets ½ inch on a lightly floured surface to form a 12x14-inch rectangle; press edges firmly to seal. Trim pastry 2½ inches longer than the length of tenderloin.

◆ Spread the mushroom mixture over the top and sides of the tenderloin. Place the tenderloin in the center of the pastry.

◆ Fold the pastry over the tenderloin; press the edges to seal. Decorate the top with any pastry trimmings.

◆ Brush the pastry with a mixture of the egg and cold water. Place in a greased 10x15-inch baking pan.

◆ Bake for 20 to 25 minutes or until the pastry is golden brown.

◆ Let stand for 10 minutes before slicing.

◆ Makes 8 to 10 servings.

Pot Roast with Roasted Root Vegetables

1 (3-pound) eye-of-round

3 tablespoons vegetable oil

Salt and pepper to taste

2 medium yellow onions

2 carrots, cut into halves

2 ribs celery, cut into halves

2 bay leaves

3 parsley sprigs

3 thyme sprigs, or 1
   teaspoon dried thyme

3 cups (about) beef stock

12 small beets

12 small carrots, peeled

12 small white onions

12 small parsnips, trimmed,
   peeled

12 small new potatoes

1 head garlic, separated
   into cloves

◆ Rinse the beef quickly under cold water; pat dry. Tie with kitchen twine if in several pieces.

◆ Brown the beef on all sides in the vegetable oil in a Dutch oven; drain. Season with salt and pepper.

◆ Add 2 yellow onions, 2 carrots, celery, bay leaves, parsley, thyme and just enough beef stock to come halfway up the sides of the beef. Bring to a boil over high heat; cover.

◆ Bake at 325 degrees for 1½ hours or until the beef is tender, continually adding additional stock to maintain approximately 2 cups of liquid in the Dutch oven at all times. Baste with the pan drippings occasionally.

◆ Remove from oven; discard the vegetables and herbs. Arrange the beets, 12 carrots, 12 white onions, parsnips, new potatoes, garlic and additional stock to come halfway up the sides of the vegetables around the roast. Cook, covered, for 30 minutes longer or until the vegetables are tender. Let stand for 15 minutes before serving.

◆ May combine the pan drippings with approximately 1 tablespoon of flour for gravy. Substitute water, cranberry juice or orange juice for the beef stock if desired. May substitute any boneless lean beef cut for the eye-of-round. May cook the roast in a countertop roaster.

◆ Makes 12 servings.

Buffalo is known for its "Beef on Weck" sandwiches, succulent sliced roast beef served on a kimmelweck roll (a roll topped with salt and caraway seeds). This sandwich is believed to have been introduced into the area by German burghers during the nineteenth century.

Niagara Falls

In 1846, the Maid of the Mist tourist attraction made its first appearance in Western New York, and still exists today. The boat is named after folklore involving a beautiful maiden.

Other noteworthy lore involved an ice jam on the Niagara River in 1848 that caused Niagara Falls to stop for thirty hours.

Not only is the area noted for its beauty but its natural resources. In 1878, Jacob F. Schoellkopf started a hydroelectric project (the Niagara Falls ➤

Steak Shaniqua

1 (12-ounce) New York strip steak

3 ounces sliced mushrooms

2 ounces chopped onion

½ teaspoon minced garlic

2 tablespoons olive oil

¼ cup white wine

5 ounces brown gravy

Salt and pepper to taste

2 slices Swiss cheese

◆ Broil or grill the steak to desired degree of doneness.

◆ Sauté the mushrooms, onion and garlic in the olive oil in a skillet for 2 minutes. Stir in the white wine.

◆ Simmer until the liquid evaporates, stirring frequently. Add the gravy and mix well. Season with salt and pepper.

◆ Simmer just until heated through, stirring constantly.

◆ Place the steak on a baking pan. Spoon the vegetable mixture over the steak. Top with the cheese.

◆ Broil until the cheese melts. Serve immediately.

◆ Makes 1 to 2 servings.

Veal with Three Mustards

This mustard sauce is equally good with boneless breast of chicken.

6 medium shallots, minced

1½ cups dry white wine

1 cup chicken stock

3½ cups whipping cream

⅓ cup tarragon mustard

⅓ cup Dijon mustard

⅓ cup Moutarde de Meaux

1 tablespoon butter

12 (3-ounce) veal cutlets

Kosher salt and freshly
ground pepper to taste

2 to 3 tablespoons butter

◆ Measure the eight ingredients for the sauce before cooking the veal. Set sauce ingredients aside until needed.

◆ Flatten the veal cutlets ¼ inch thick between sheets of waxed paper. Season both sides of the cutlets with kosher salt and pepper.

◆ Heat 1 tablespoon of the butter in a large skillet over medium heat until hot; do not allow to burn.

◆ Sauté the veal in batches in the hot butter for 2 minutes per side, adding the remaining 1 to 2 tablespoons butter as needed.

◆ Transfer the veal to a heated platter; tent with foil to keep warm.

◆ Sauté the shallots in the pan drippings over medium heat until tender. Stir in the white wine and stock. Increase the heat to high.

◆ Cook until of a syrupy consistency, stirring constantly. Reduce the heat to medium-low. Stir in the whipping cream.

◆ Cook until the mixture is of a sauce consistency, stirring constantly. Whisk in the tarragon mustard, Dijon mustard and Moutarde de Meaux; do not allow to boil. Add additional whipping cream if sauce is too thick. Swirl in 1 tablespoon butter, stirring until blended.

◆ Arrange the veal on individual dinner plates; top with the sauce.

◆ Makes 6 servings.

Hydroelectric Power & Manufacturing Company), which became the greatest of its kind in the world. Fifty percent of the Niagara River is diverted during evening hours from going over the Falls to power hydro-electric plants, during the tourist season.

In 1966, the local branch of the United States Army Corps of Engineers achieved fame by "turning off" Niagara Falls.

The Falls is a part of the Niagara River, the fastest river in the Western Hemisphere.

Western New York's Hollywood Connection

The following people have been born in or lived in the area:
Kim Alexis
Lucille Ball
Amanda Blake
Diane English
Tom Fontana
Aretha Franklin
Shannon Gaughan
Joey Giambra
Patrick Hasburgh
Beverly Johnson
Nancy Marchand
Jack Parr
John Schenk
James Whitmore ➤

Veal in Wine Sauce with Spätzle

2 pounds veal stew meat

1 medium onion, chopped

6 tablespoons butter

⅓ cup plus 2 tablespoons flour

3 cups water

1 tablespoon chicken bouillon

1 bay leaf

20 whole cloves

1 teaspoon black peppercorns

½ cup dry white wine

2 (¼-inch) lemon slices

¼ teaspoon nutmeg

½ teaspoon crushed garlic

12 ounces fresh whole mushrooms

Spätzle (page 83)

◆ Place the stew meat in a large colander. Pour boiling water over the veal, tossing until the veal is white in color. This seals in the juices.

◆ Sauté the onion in the butter in a 6-quart saucepan until tender; do not brown. Sift the flour over the onion mixture; whisk until mixed. Add the water and bouillon gradually, whisking constantly. Cook until thickened, whisking constantly.

◆ Place the bay leaf, cloves and peppercorns in a cheesecloth pouch. Add to the sauce. Add the veal and white wine and mix well.

◆ Simmer over low heat for 1 hour, stirring occasionally. Add the lemon slices, nutmeg, garlic and mushrooms.

◆ Cook for 1 hour longer or until the veal is tender, stirring occasionally. Discard the cheesecloth pouch.

◆ Serve with or spoon over the Spätzle.

◆ Makes 4 to 6 servings.

➤

Spätzle

4 cups flour

4 eggs

1 teaspoon nutmeg

½ teaspoon salt

8 to 10 tablespoons water

◆ Mix the flour, eggs, nutmeg and salt in a bowl with a wooden spoon. Add the water gradually, stirring until mixed; dough should be thick and stretchy.

◆ Place a small amount of the dough on a damp wooden board; cut into slivers with a knife.

◆ Drop the dough slivers in small batches into boiling water in a stockpot. Cook until the spätzle floats to the surface; remove with a slotted spoon to a heated bowl. Repeat the process in batches with the remaining dough.

◆ May be served plain with butter and parsley or in your favorite sauce.

◆ Makes 4 to 6 servings.

The following movies have been filmed in the area:

Best Friends

Hide in Plain Sight

My Dark Lady

The Natural

Trains, Planes, and Automobiles

Veal Shanks with Capers

1½ cups buttermilk

¼ cup fresh lemon juice

3 cloves of garlic, minced

1 tablespoon pepper

3 pounds (1-inch) veal
    shanks

2 tablespoons olive oil

2 tablespoons butter

4 leeks, cut lengthwise into
    ¼-inch strips

2 cups dry white wine

1 tablespoon capers

Salt and pepper to taste

◆ Combine the buttermilk, lemon juice, garlic and 1 tablespoon pepper in a bowl and mix well. Add the veal shanks, tossing to coat.

◆ Marinate the shanks for 1 to 2 hours at room temperature or for 8 to 10 hours in the refrigerator, turning occasionally. Drain, reserving the marinade. Pat the shanks dry.

◆ Heat the olive oil and butter in a heavy pan. Cook the shanks on both sides until brown. Remove to a platter.

◆ Sauté the leeks in the pan drippings until light brown, adding additional olive oil and butter if necessary. Stir in the white wine and reserved marinade. Bring to a boil; reduce heat. Return the shanks to the pan.

◆ Simmer, covered, for 1 hour. Stir in the capers.

◆ Simmer for 30 minutes longer, stirring occasionally. Season with salt and pepper to taste. Garnish with a mixture of garlic, parsley and lemon peel.

◆ Makes 6 servings.

Buffalo was the first city in the country to light streets with electricity.

Pork Medallions au Poivre

1½ pounds pork tenderloin

Salt and pepper to taste

3 tablespoons butter or
   margarine

3 shallots, minced

½ cup dry vermouth

1½ cups chicken stock

1 tablespoon drained green
   peppercorns in brine

1½ teaspoons minced fresh
   thyme

2 teaspoons Dijon mustard

½ cup whipping cream

---

*Dijon mustard originated
in the French city of Dijon.
It is a result of combining
spices, white wine, and
mustard.*

◆ Cut the pork into sixteen 1-inch medallions; flatten slightly with palm of hand. Season with salt and pepper.

◆ Heat 2 tablespoons of the butter in a large heavy skillet over medium-high heat until melted. Add the pork.

◆ Cook for 3 minutes per side or until brown, stirring frequently. Transfer the pork to a platter.

◆ Heat the remaining 1 tablespoon butter with the pan drippings in the skillet until the butter melts. Add the shallots. Sauté for 2 minutes. Stir in the vermouth. Bring to a boil.

◆ Boil for 5 minutes or until reduced to the consistency of a glaze, stirring frequently. Stir in the stock, peppercorns and thyme. Bring to a boil.

◆ Boil for 10 minutes or until reduced to ¼ cup. Whisk in the Dijon mustard; whisk in the whipping cream. Season with salt and pepper. Return the pork and any juices to the skillet.

◆ Simmer for 3 minutes or until the pork is cooked through and the sauce thickens slightly, stirring constantly.

◆ Spoon the pork medallions and sauce onto dinner plates. Garnish with additional minced fresh thyme.

◆ Makes 4 servings.

---

*Buffalo was the first city
in the state to implement
free public schools.*

Currant Mustard Pork Tenderloin

4 whole pork tenderloins, trimmed

Freshly ground pepper

1½ to 3 teaspoons butter

1½ cups dry white wine

¾ cup currant jelly

½ cup Dijon mustard

1 tablespoon dried currants

½ teaspoon thyme

◆ Season the tenderloins liberally with pepper.

◆ Heat the butter in a skillet over medium-high heat until melted. Add the tenderloins.

◆ Sauté for 5 minutes or until brown on all sides. Arrange the tenderloins in a roasting pan.

◆ Deglaze the skillet with the white wine.

◆ Heat the jelly in a saucepan until melted. Whisk in the Dijon mustard until blended. Stir into the white wine mixture. Add the currants and thyme and mix well. Pour over the pork.

◆ Bake at 325 degrees for 50 minutes or until cooked through, basting frequently.

◆ Remove the tenderloins from the sauce to a platter. Cut diagonally into slices.

◆ Spoon the sauce onto individual dinner plates; top with sliced tenderloin. Garnish with fresh thyme sprigs.

◆ Makes 6 servings.

Gregory Jarvis, an astronaut aboard the space shuttle Challenger, graduated from the University of Buffalo.

Herb-Crusted Lamb and Potatoes

*Serve with green beans tossed with Roquefort cheese,
green salad and Cabernet Sauvignon.*

1 (7- to 8-pound) leg of
    lamb

2 large cloves of garlic,
    slivered

5 tablespoons olive oil

2 tablespoons plus
    2 teaspoons thyme

2 tablespoons dried
    rosemary

2 tablespoons plus
    1 teaspoon coarsely
    ground pepper

2 teaspoons coriander

30 new potatoes, cut into
    quarters

1 teaspoon kosher salt

Rosemary sprigs

------

*Coriander seeds, white and
lemon-flavored, resemble
peppercorns. These seeds,
either ground or whole,
are used in curries, soups,
stews, stir-fry dishes, or
desserts. Coriander leaves,
also commonly known as
cilantro, are used in a
variety of highly seasoned
dishes.*

◆ Cut slits in lamb; place garlic slivers in
the slits. Brush with 2 tablespoons of
the olive oil.

◆ Combine 2 tablespoons thyme, 2 tablespoons dried rosemary, 2 tablespoons
pepper and coriander in a bowl and
mix well. Pat the herb mixture evenly
over the lamb. Arrange the lamb in a
shallow roasting pan.

◆ Combine the new potatoes, remaining
3 tablespoons olive oil, remaining
2 teaspoons thyme, remaining 1
teaspoon pepper, kosher salt and
rosemary sprigs in a bowl, tossing
to coat. Arrange the potatoes around
the lamb.

◆ Roast at 325 degrees for 3 to 4 hours
or until a meat thermometer inserted
in the thickest part of the leg registers
120 degrees for rare or until done
to taste, stirring the potatoes every
30 minutes.

◆ Tent the lamb with foil. Let stand for
15 minutes. Slice as desired.

◆ Makes 8 servings.

Grilled Lamb Chops with Gorgonzola Butter

16 (1½- to 2-inch) lamb chops

1 cup olive oil

8 shallots, finely chopped

¼ cup chopped garlic

4 teaspoons dried crumbled rosemary

Gorgonzola Butter (below)

◆ Pat the lamb chops dry with a paper towel. Arrange in a 9x13-inch glass dish.

◆ Whisk the olive oil, shallots, garlic and rosemary in a bowl or process in a food processor until mixed. Pour over the lamb chops, turning to coat.

◆ Marinate in the refrigerator for 3 to 10 hours, turning occasionally. Drain, discarding the marinade. Let stand until room temperature.

◆ Grill the lamb chops over hot coals for 6 minutes per side for medium-rare or until done to taste.

◆ Arrange 2 lamb chops on each dinner plate. Top each lamb chop with a Gorgonzola Butter patty.

◆ Makes 8 servings.

Gorgonzola Butter

1 cup butter, softened

6 ounces Gorgonzola cheese, softened

2 tablespoons olive oil

2 tablespoons fresh lemon juice

4 teaspoons minced shallots

2 teaspoons minced garlic

½ teaspoon each kosher salt and freshly ground pepper (optional)

◆ Combine the butter, Gorgonzola cheese, olive oil, lemon juice, shallots, garlic, kosher salt and pepper in a bowl and mix well.

◆ Shape the mixture into 16 patties, approximately 1 inch in diameter and ¹/₂ inch thick. Wrap in plastic wrap.

◆ Freeze for 3 hours or up to 1 week in advance.

◆ Makes 1³/₄ cups.

Greek Marinated Kabobs

This recipe is also excellent with chicken or beef.

½ cup olive oil

¼ cup lemon juice

¼ cup minced fresh parsley

1 small onion, chopped

1 clove of garlic, minced

1 teaspoon salt

1 teaspoon thyme

1 teaspoon marjoram

½ teaspoon pepper

¼ teaspoon celery seeds

8 ounces lamb, cut into
    1-inch pieces

Whole mushrooms

Onions, cut into wedges

Green bell peppers, cut into
    wedges

Carrots, cut into chunks

◆ Combine the olive oil, lemon juice, parsley, chopped onion, garlic, salt, thyme, marjoram, pepper and celery seeds in a bowl and mix well. Pour over the lamb in a shallow dish, turning to coat.

◆ Marinate, covered, in the refrigerator for 8 to 10 hours, turning occasionally. Drain, reserving the marinade.

◆ Thread the lamb, mushrooms, onion wedges, green peppers and carrots alternately on skewers.

◆ Grill over hot coals until the lamb is done to taste and the vegetables are of the desired degree of crispness, turning and basting occasionally with the reserved marinade.

◆ Makes 3 to 4 servings.

Abbott and Costello began their long-lasting comic partnership during a show in Buffalo's Gayety Theatre in 1930.

Herb-Marinated Lamb

1 (5- to 6-pound) leg of lamb, butterflied

½ cup olive oil

½ cup lemon juice

¼ cup chopped onion

3 cloves of garlic, minced

1 tablespoon Worcestershire sauce

½ teaspoon ground pepper

½ teaspoon dried thyme

◆ Place the leg of lamb in a nonreactive dish.

◆ Combine the olive oil, lemon juice, onion, garlic, Worcestershire sauce, pepper and thyme in a bowl and mix well. Pour over the lamb, turning to coat.

◆ Marinate in the refrigerator for 3 to 10 hours, turning occasionally. Drain, reserving the marinade.

◆ Grill the lamb over hot coals for 40 to 45 minutes or until done to taste, basting with the reserved marinade occasionally.

◆ Makes 12 to 15 servings.

Chinese Fried Chicken Wings

20 to 25 chicken wings

3 teaspoons salt

2 cups flour

¼ teaspoon pepper

½ teaspoon cornstarch

2 cups water

¼ cup peanut oil

1 egg, beaten

Vegetable oil for deep-frying

◆ Rinse the chicken wings and pat dry. Sprinkle with 1 teaspoon of the salt.

◆ Combine 1 cup of the flour, 1 teaspoon of the salt and pepper in a food storage bag and mix well. Add the chicken, shaking to coat.

◆ Combine the remaining 1 cup flour, remaining 1 teaspoon salt and cornstarch in a bowl and mix well. Stir in the water, peanut oil and egg. Coat the floured chicken with the egg mixture.

◆ Heat the vegetable oil in a skillet to 400 degrees. Deep-fry the chicken in the hot oil until golden brown on all sides; drain.

◆ Makes 20 to 25 chicken wings.

Buffalo Chicken Wings

20 to 25 chicken wings

Vegetable oil for deep-frying

¼ cup melted butter or margarine

Hot sauce

Bleu Cheese Dressing (below)

Celery sticks

◆ Disjoint the chicken wings and discard the tips. Rinse and pat dry. The wings must be completely dry to fry properly since there is no batter or breading.

◆ Preheat the oil in a deep fryer or a large deep pan to 365 degrees.

◆ Add the chicken wings a few at a time to the hot oil. Do not allow the oil to cool as the chicken is added. Deep-fry for 6 to 10 minutes or until crisp and golden brown. Drain well by shaking in the fryer basket or a strainer.

◆ Blend the butter with ½ bottle of hot sauce for medium-hot wings. Add additional hot sauce for hotter wings or additional butter for milder wings.

◆ Combine the wings and the hot sauce in a large container. Let stand, covered.

◆ Serve the chicken wings with Bleu Cheese Dressing and celery sticks.

◆ Makes 20 to 25 chicken wings.

Bleu Cheese Dressing

2 cups mayonnaise

3 tablespoons cider vinegar

½ teaspoon dry mustard

½ teaspoon white pepper

¼ teaspoon salt

8 ounces bleu cheese, crumbled

¼ to ½ cup cold water

◆ Combine the mayonnaise, vinegar, dry mustard, pepper and salt in a large bowl and beat until well blended. Mix in the bleu cheese.

◆ Add enough cold water gradually to make the dressing of the desired consistency, whisking constantly.

◆ Store in an airtight container in the refrigerator.

◆ Makes 3½ cups.

The Anchor Bar

The origin of the culinary delight known as "chicken wings" began one Friday night in 1964 at Buffalo's Anchor Bar, owned by Frank and Teressa Bellissimo. Friends of the Bellissimo family had stopped at the bar for a late-night snack. While fixing the snack Teressa was about to put chicken wings into a stockpot for soup when she thought "It's a shame to put such beautiful wings into a stockpot." The rest is history!

Curry-Glazed Sesame Wings

¼ cup sesame seeds

½ cup honey

¼ cup prepared mustard

2 tablespoons melted butter
   or margarine

1 teaspoon salt

1 teaspoon curry powder

12 chicken wings, whole or
   separated into joints

◆ Spread the sesame seeds in a shallow baking pan. Bake at 350 degrees for 10 minutes or until golden brown. May spread in a microwave-safe dish and microwave on High for 6 minutes or until golden brown, stirring once or twice.

◆ Combine the honey, prepared mustard, butter, salt and curry powder in a bowl, stirring until blended.

◆ Rinse the chicken and pat dry. Arrange in a broiler pan.

◆ Broil 4 inches from heat source for 20 minutes for whole wings or 10 minutes for sectioned chicken wings, turning once, or grill chicken wings over medium-hot coals. Baste with the honey mixture.

◆ Broil for 10 to 20 minutes longer or until the chicken is cooked through, turning and basting occasionally.

◆ Dip the chicken wings in the sesame seeds; arrange on a serving platter.

During the Blizzard of 1977, three-thousand-five-hundred automobiles were stranded on Erie County streets.

Gingered Chicken Wings

12 chicken wings, whole or
    separated into joints

⅓ cup soy sauce

¼ cup lightly packed brown
    sugar

3 tablespoons finely
    chopped candied ginger

2 tablespoons vinegar

1 tablespoon cornstarch

1 large clove of garlic,
    minced or pressed

◆───────◆

One tablespoon of finely
chopped fresh gingerroot
may be substituted for 3
tablespoons of finely
chopped candied ginger.

◆ Rinse the chicken and pat dry. Arrange
in a shallow dish.

◆ Combine the soy sauce, brown sugar,
ginger, vinegar, cornstarch and garlic in
a bowl and mix well. Pour over the
chicken, turning to coat.

◆ Marinate, covered, in the refrigerator
for 1 to 4 hours, turning occasionally.
Drain, reserving the marinade.

◆ Arrange the chicken in a broiler pan.
Broil 4 inches from heat source for 15
to 20 minutes or grill the chicken
approximately 6 inches above hot
coals until cooked through, turning
and basting with the reserved
marinade occasionally.

*Buffalonian C. Roy
Keys developed and tested
the hydroplane in 1928.*

Almond-Orange Chicken

6 boneless skinless chicken
  breasts

5 tablespoons orange juice

3 tablespoons Dijon
  mustard

1 tablespoon grated orange
  peel

¼ teaspoon black pepper

2 cloves of garlic, chopped

6½ tablespoons olive oil

1 cup sliced almonds

2 cups chicken broth

1 tablespoon cornstarch

1 tablespoon water

2 tablespoons orange
  marmalade

2 tablespoons chopped fresh
  parsley

¼ teaspoon red pepper
  flakes

6 orange slices

◆ Rinse the chicken and pat dry. Arrange in a shallow dish.

◆ Combine the orange juice, Dijon mustard, orange peel, black pepper and garlic in a bowl and mix well. Whisk in 5 tablespoons of the olive oil. Pour over the chicken, turning to coat.

◆ Marinate in the refrigerator for 1 hour, turning occasionally.

◆ Sauté the almonds in ½ tablespoon of the olive oil in a skillet until golden brown. Remove to a bowl.

◆ Drain the chicken, reserving the marinade.

◆ Sauté the chicken in the remaining 1 tablespoon olive oil in a skillet for 6 to 10 minutes per side or until brown and cooked through, turning occasionally. Remove the chicken to a platter. Strain the reserved marinade into the pan drippings in the skillet. Add the broth and a mixture of the cornstarch and water and mix well.

◆ Cook over high heat for 5 minutes or until reduced by half, stirring constantly. Stir in the marmalade.

◆ Cook until blended, stirring constantly. Stir in the parsley and red pepper flakes. Return the chicken to the skillet.

◆ Cook until the chicken is heated through, stirring constantly.

◆ Arrange 1 chicken breast on each plate; top with an orange slice. Sprinkle with the almonds. Serve with the sauce.

◆ Makes 6 servings.

Chicken with Balsamic Vinegar and Mushrooms

6 boneless skinless chicken
   breast halves

2 tablespoons flour

Ground pepper to taste

1 tablespoon olive oil

16 ounces assorted
   mushrooms, chopped

2 shallots, minced

1 cup chicken broth

¼ cup balsamic vinegar

¼ cup white wine

¼ teaspoon thyme

1 bay leaf

Balsamic vinegar is brown in color, has a fruity aroma and a sweet-and-sour flavor. True balsamic vinegar is aged for fifty to two hundred years, being passed down from generation to generation. It is only produced in Emilia-Romagna, a region of Northern Italy. Industrialized balsamic vinegar that is available in grocery stores is generally aged for three years and is labeled aceto balsamico.

◆ Rinse the chicken and pat dry. Coat with a mixture of the flour and pepper.

◆ Sauté the chicken in the olive oil in a skillet until light brown on both sides. Remove the chicken with a slotted spoon to a platter. Tent with foil to keep warm.

◆ Sauté the mushrooms and shallots in the pan drippings for 3 minutes. Stir in the broth, balsamic vinegar, white wine, thyme and bay leaf. Return the chicken to the skillet.

◆ Cook, covered, over medium-low heat for 10 minutes or until the chicken is cooked through, turning the chicken once. Transfer the chicken to a serving platter; cover to keep warm.

◆ Cook the mushroom mixture over medium heat for 5 to 7 minutes or until reduced to the desired consistency, stirring constantly. Discard the bay leaf. Pour the sauce over the chicken. Serve with hot cooked rice or pasta.

◆ Makes 6 servings.

Chicken Breasts with Mustard Seed Sauce

6 whole chicken breasts,
   split, boned

½ teaspoon salt

½ teaspoon pepper

8 ounces mushrooms, sliced

1 tablespoon melted butter

Mustard Seed Sauce (below)

◆ Rinse the chicken and pat dry. Arrange skin side up in a baking pan. Season with the salt and pepper.

◆ Bake at 500 degrees for 12 minutes or just until there is a trace of pink in the center.

◆ Broil for 1 minute or until the skin is brown and crispy and the chicken is cooked through. Sauté the mushrooms in the butter in a skillet.

◆ Arrange the chicken on a serving platter; top with the mushrooms. Spoon the Mustard Seed Sauce over the top.

◆ Makes 12 servings.

Wells Fargo was formed by two men in Buffalo in the early 1800s as an express service to and from the West.

Mustard Seed Sauce

1½ tablespoons mustard
   seeds

1 cup whipping cream

1 cup half-and-half

3½ tablespoons Dijon
   mustard

½ teaspoon pepper

¼ teaspoon salt

2 teaspoons lemon juice

3 scallions, chopped

◆ Toast the mustard seeds in a skillet over medium-high heat until light brown and the seeds begin to pop, shaking the pan frequently. Remove to a platter to cool.

◆ Combine the whipping cream and half-and-half in a saucepan. Bring to a boil; reduce heat.

◆ Cook for 10 minutes or until reduced to 1¼ cups, stirring occasionally. Remove from heat. Whisk in the Dijon mustard, pepper and salt.

◆ Stir the mustard seeds, lemon juice and scallions into the sauce just before serving.

◆ Makes 12 servings.

Fruit-Glazed Chicken

4 boneless skinless chicken
   breast halves

2 tablespoons butter

1½ cups orange marmalade

8 ounces dried currants

½ cup applesauce

½ cup orange juice

4 ounces dried apricots

⅓ cup packed brown sugar

1 teaspoon pepper

1 teaspoon dry mustard

◆ Rinse the chicken and pat dry.

◆ Sauté the chicken in the butter in a
   skillet until brown on all sides. Arrange
   in a 9x14-inch baking pan.

◆ Combine the marmalade, currants,
   applesauce, orange juice, apricots,
   brown sugar, pepper and dry mustard
   in a saucepan and mix well.

◆ Cook over low heat until heated
   through, stirring constantly. Pour over
   the chicken.

◆ Bake, covered with foil, at 350 degrees
   for 1 hour; remove foil.

◆ Broil for 3 to 5 minutes or until bubbly.

◆ Makes 4 servings.

Grilled Bourbon Chicken

4 chicken breast halves

⅓ cup bourbon

⅓ cup Dijon mustard

⅓ cup packed brown sugar

⅓ cup soy sauce

⅓ cup chopped scallions

1 tablespoon Worcestershire
   sauce

½ teaspoon pepper

◆ Rinse the chicken and pat dry. Arrange
   in a shallow dish.

◆ Combine the bourbon, Dijon mustard,
   brown sugar, soy sauce, scallions,
   Worcestershire sauce and pepper in a
   bowl and mix well. Spoon over the
   chicken, turning to coat.

◆ Marinate, covered, in the refrigerator
   for 24 hours, turning frequently. Drain,
   discarding marinade.

◆ Grill the chicken over hot coals for 25
   minutes or until cooked through,
   turning occasionally.

◆ Makes 4 servings.

Chicken Piccata

Serve with rice pilaf and a green salad.

6 boneless skinless chicken
   breast halves

Salt and pepper to taste

Juice of 1 lemon

Flour

1/3 to 1/2 cup butter

1/2 cup dry white wine

Glaze baked chicken or turkey with a simple tasty sauce of one 16-ounce can of jellied cranberry sauce melted with 1/2 cup pineapple juice and brushed over the poultry thirty minutes before the end of the cooking process.

◆ Rinse the chicken and pat dry. Pound the chicken as thin as possible between sheets of waxed paper using a meat mallet.

◆ Arrange the chicken in a dish. Season with salt and pepper; drizzle with lemon juice.

◆ Chill for 10 minutes or longer. Coat the chicken with flour.

◆ Sauté the chicken in the butter in a large nonstick skillet over high heat for 7 minutes per side; reduce heat.

◆ Cook until tender, turning occasionally. Transfer the chicken to a heated platter.

◆ Stir the wine into the pan drippings. Bring to a boil. Pour over the chicken.

◆ Makes 4 to 6 servings.

Sunday Chicken

6 to 8 fresh or frozen
   broccoli spears

6 to 8 cling peach halves

3 whole chicken breasts,
   split, skinned

Salt and freshly ground
   pepper to taste

½ cup melted butter

1 teaspoon paprika

1 clove of garlic, crushed

1 cup sour cream

¼ cup mayonnaise

⅓ cup grated Parmesan
   cheese

◆ Cook the broccoli with a small amount of water in a saucepan until tender-crisp; drain.

◆ Drain the peach halves on paper towels; pat dry.

◆ Rinse the chicken and pat dry. Season with salt and pepper.

◆ Combine the butter, paprika and garlic in a baking dish. Add the chicken, turning to coat.

◆ Bake, loosely covered with foil, at 375 degrees for 30 minutes. Combine the sour cream and mayonnaise in a bowl and mix well. Coat the chicken with ½ of the mixture.

◆ Bake, loosely covered with foil, for 20 minutes longer or until the chicken is cooked through. Arrange the broccoli and peaches around the chicken; spread with the remaining sour cream mixture.

◆ Sprinkle with the Parmesan cheese. Place on the bottom oven rack.

◆ Broil until glazed and light brown.

◆ Makes 6 servings.

In 1981, Charlie Chapman of Buffalo was the first black American to swim the English Channel.

Sherry Chicken for a Crowd

6 whole chicken breasts,
  split, boned

Paprika to taste

Salt and pepper to taste

½ cup butter

2 (15-ounce) cans
  artichokes, drained,
  sliced

16 ounces fresh mushrooms,
  trimmed, sliced

¼ teaspoon tarragon

6 tablespoons flour

3 cups chicken broth

¾ cup cooking sherry

---

*Tarragon grows to over
three feet in height and has
narrow, dark green leaves
with tiny yellow flowers. It
is best used fresh and can
enhance the flavor of
chicken, fish, vegetables,
or vinegars. Tarragon is
easily bruised, so handle
this herb gently.*

◆ Rinse the chicken and pat dry. Season with paprika, salt and pepper.

◆ Sauté the chicken in ¼ cup of the butter in a skillet until brown on both sides. Arrange the chicken in a 9x13-inch baking dish. Top with the artichokes.

◆ Sauté the mushrooms and tarragon in the remaining ¼ cup butter in a skillet for 5 minutes. Sprinkle with the flour. Stir in the broth and sherry.

◆ Simmer for 5 minutes, stirring occasionally. Pour over the chicken and artichokes. (The dish may be prepared to this point and stored in the refrigerator until just before baking.)

◆ Bake, covered, at 350 degrees for 45 minutes or until the chicken is cooked through.

◆ Makes 12 servings.

Italian Sausage-Stuffed Squash

Suit your taste . . . use mild, medium or HOT sausage. Great for a cold wintry day with a salad and hot crusty bread.

2 acorn squash

4 tablespoons margarine, softened

4 tablespoons brown sugar

1 large onion, chopped

1 medium green bell pepper, chopped

1 medium red bell pepper, chopped

4 Italian poultry sausage links, crumbled

◆ Cut the acorn squash lengthwise into halves; discard the seeds.

◆ Spread each half with ½ tablespoon of the margarine; sprinkle each half with 1 tablespoon brown sugar. Place in a baking dish or individual baking dishes.

◆ Bake at 350 degrees for 1 hour or until the squash pulp is tender enough to be scooped out.

◆ Sauté the onion and bell peppers while the squash bakes in the remaining 2 tablespoons of margarine in a skillet for 5 to 10 minutes or until the onion is tender. Remove the onion mixture with a slotted spoon to a bowl.

◆ Brown the sausage in the pan drippings in the skillet; skim off fat. Stir in the onion mixture.

◆ Scoop the squash pulp into the sausage mixture, being careful to leave the squash shells intact. Stuff each squash shell with ¼ of the sausage mixture. Place in a baking dish.

◆ Bake for 15 minutes longer.

◆ May be prepared in advance, stored in the refrigerator, and reheated for the last 15 minutes just before serving.

◆ Makes 4 servings.

The region we now call Buffalo was originally known as New Amsterdam.

Barbecued Duck Breasts on Sweet Corn Pancakes

This barbecue sauce is also excellent on chicken, pork or beef.

4 boneless duck breasts,
    trimmed

1 tablespoon minced garlic

1 tablespoon minced shallot

1 tablespoon minced
    gingerroot

1 tablespoon sesame oil

½ cup soy sauce

½ cup barbecue sauce

¼ cup hoisin sauce

¼ cup packed brown sugar

¼ cup rice wine vinegar

Sweet Corn Pancakes
    (page 103)

◆ Rinse the duck and pat dry.

◆ Sauté the garlic, shallot and gingerroot in the sesame oil in a saucepan. Add the soy sauce, barbecue sauce, hoisin sauce, brown sugar and wine vinegar and mix well.

◆ Simmer for 10 minutes, stirring occasionally. Let stand until cool. Brush the duck with the barbecue sauce.

◆ This barbecue sauce may be prepared in advance and stored in the refrigerator for up to 4 weeks.

◆ Grill the duck over hot coals or broil for 8 to 10 minutes or until cooked through, basting with the sauce frequently. Let stand for 4 to 5 minutes before slicing.

◆ Place the Sweet Corn Pancakes on 4 dinner plates. Cut the duck cross grain into thin slices. Arrange over the pancakes.

◆ Bring the remaining sauce to a boil; drizzle the sauce around the outer edge of the plate.

◆ Makes 4 servings.

Sweet Corn Pancakes

1 pound frozen corn,
  thawed

2 eggs

¼ cup finely chopped onion

2 scallions, finely chopped

1 clove of garlic, minced

¾ cup flour

¼ cup cornmeal

1 tablespoon baking powder

1½ teaspoons salt

1½ teaspoons sugar

1½ teaspoons crushed red
  pepper

Vegetable oil for frying

◆ Process ½ of the corn in a food processor until puréed. Mix with the remaining corn, eggs, onion, scallions and garlic.

◆ Combine the flour, cornmeal, baking powder, salt, sugar and red pepper in a bowl and mix well. Stir in the corn mixture.

◆ Chill, covered, in the refrigerator.

◆ Heat a small amount of oil in a nonstick skillet. Pour enough batter into the skillet to form a 3- to 4-inch pancake.

◆ Bake until brown on both sides, turning once. Repeat the process with the remaining batter.

◆ May prepare pancakes in advance, store in the refrigerator and reheat in the oven just before serving.

◆ Makes 4 servings.

Red Jacket, a Seneca chief buried at Forest Lawn Cemetery in Buffalo, was so named because he sided with the British during the American Revolutionary War. Red Jacket was a great spokesman for his people.

*The Buffalo Zoo
is one of the oldest in
the United States.*

Crab Cakes

2 pounds crab meat

½ cup bread crumbs

¼ cup mayonnaise

*3 green onions, finely
chopped*

2 ribs celery, finely chopped

2 eggs, beaten

*4 teaspoons Worcestershire
sauce*

*1 tablespoon horseradish,
drained*

1 tablespoon Dijon mustard

*2 teaspoons Old Bay
seasoning*

1 teaspoon pepper

½ teaspoon salt (optional)

½ teaspoon parsley flakes

⅛ teaspoon Tabasco sauce

◆ Combine the crab meat, bread crumbs, mayonnaise, green onions, celery, eggs, Worcestershire sauce, horseradish, Dijon mustard, Old Bay seasoning, pepper, salt, parsley flakes and Tabasco sauce in a bowl and mix well. Shape into 12 large patties. Place on a baking sheet.

◆ Chill, covered, until just before serving time.

◆ Bake at 500 degrees for 10 to 15 minutes on each side or until brown, turning once.

◆ Serve immediately with lemon slices, tartar sauce or Seafood Sauce on page 105.

◆ Makes 6 servings.

Seafood Sauce

1/4 cup sun-dried tomatoes

1 cup mayonnaise

2 hard-cooked eggs,
    chopped

2 tablespoons julienned
    fresh basil leaves

2 tablespoons Pinot Grigio
    or other white wine

1 tablespoon fresh thyme
    leaves

1 tablespoon fresh oregano
    leaves

1 tablespoon barbecue
    sauce

1 tablespoon Dijon mustard

2 cloves of garlic, finely
    minced

Juice of 1 lemon

Tabasco sauce to taste

◆ Rehydrate the sun-dried tomatoes in
   a small amount of water in a bowl.
   Drain and julienne.

◆ Combine the sun-dried tomatoes,
   mayonnaise, eggs, basil, wine, thyme,
   oregano, barbecue sauce, Dijon
   mustard, garlic, lemon juice and
   Tabasco sauce in a bowl and mix well.

◆ Chill, covered, until serving time.

◆ Serve with hot or cold seafood of
   your choice.

◆ Makes 1¾ cups.

Lobster Ginger

1 quart water

½ cup white wine

1 carrot, finely chopped

1 rib celery, finely chopped

1 (1¼-pound) lobster

4 ounces fresh spinach, trimmed

2 tablespoons butter

Salt and white pepper to taste

6 tablespoons sauterne or dessert white wine

Juice of 1 lime

1 ounce gingerroot, finely chopped

½ cup unsalted butter

♦ Bring the water, ½ cup white wine, carrot and celery to a boil in a stockpot. Add the lobster; reduce heat.

♦ Simmer for 10 minutes; drain. Remove the meat from the shell, discarding the shell. Slice the lobster tail into 4 medallions.

♦ Sauté the spinach in 2 tablespoons butter in a sauté pan until wilted. Season with salt and white pepper.

♦ Combine 6 tablespoons sauterne, lime juice and gingerroot in a saucepan.

♦ Cook over medium-high heat until reduced by ½, stirring frequently. Whisk in ½ cup butter 1 tablespoon at a time. Season with salt and white pepper.

♦ Spoon the spinach onto a dinner plate. Arrange the lobster medallions over the spinach. Place the whole claw meat on the right and left side of the bed of spinach symbolizing the lobster. Drizzle the ginger sauce over the lobster. Serve immediately.

♦ Makes 1 serving.

Fisher Price, a division of Mattel, Inc. was founded in East Aurora, a suburb of Buffalo. Fisher Price is the world's largest maker of infant and preschool toys.

Coquilles St. Jacques

1 pound bay scallops

¾ cup water

2 tablespoons dry white
    wine

¼ to ½ teaspoon salt

⅛ teaspoon cayenne

8 ounces mushrooms, sliced

1 small onion, minced

Melted butter

¼ cup flour

½ clove of garlic, minced

1 tablespoon chopped fresh
    parsley

⅓ cup bread crumbs

2 tablespoons freshly grated
    Parmesan cheese

◆ Combine the scallops, water, white wine, salt and cayenne in a saucepan. Bring to a boil over high heat; reduce heat.

◆ Simmer for 2 minutes, stirring occasionally. Drain, reserving the liquid and scallops.

◆ Sauté the mushrooms and onion in hot melted butter in a skillet until tender. Add the flour, garlic and parsley, stirring until mixed. Add the reserved liquid gradually and mix well.

◆ Cook until thickened, stirring constantly. Add the scallops and mix gently. Spoon into greased ramekins or shells. Sprinkle with the bread crumbs and cheese.

◆ Bake at 400 degrees for 8 to 10 minutes or until bubbly.

◆ Makes 4 to 8 servings.

What once was a U.S. Post Office building spanning a complete city block is now a renovated branch of the Erie County Community College, and a major step towards revitalization of downtown Buffalo.

Crab-Stuffed Shrimp

4 ounces fresh mushrooms, finely chopped

2 tablespoons butter

1 pound crab meat, flaked

½ cup dry sherry

1 hard-cooked egg, chopped

3 scallions, finely chopped

2 tablespoons minced fresh parsley

½ teaspoon oregano

Salt and pepper to taste

1 cup fresh bread crumbs

1½ cups (about) whipping cream

20 large shrimp, peeled, deveined, butterflied

½ cup freshly grated Parmesan cheese

6 tablespoons melted butter

◆ Sauté the mushrooms in 2 tablespoons butter in a skillet until the liquid evaporates. Stir in the crab meat. Add the sherry, egg, scallions, parsley, oregano, salt, pepper and bread crumbs.

◆ Cook, uncovered, for about 2 minutes or until the sherry is steamed out. Remove from heat. Stir in just enough whipping cream to bind the mixture.

◆ Stuff each shrimp with a portion of the crab meat mixture. Arrange the shrimp stuffed side up in a baking dish. Sprinkle with the Parmesan cheese and drizzle with 6 tablespoons melted butter.

◆ Bake at 350 degrees for 15 minutes.

◆ Makes 4 servings.

When purchasing fresh crab meat, call your favorite fish market early in the morning. If you have to purchase frozen crab meat because fresh is not available, it will be thawed by the time you pick it up.

Shrimp Laurine

2 to 3 quarts water

40 jumbo shrimp

2 cups drained canned
  Italian plum tomatoes,
  cut into quarters

¼ cup white wine

3 tablespoons vegetable oil

1 tablespoon basil

1 tablespoon oregano

2 teaspoons red pepper
  flakes

1 clove of garlic, minced

8 ounces French feta cheese,
  crumbled

1 pound angel hair pasta,
  cooked, drained

◆ Bring 2 to 3 quarts of water to a boil in a stockpot. Add the shrimp.

◆ Boil for 2 to 3 minutes or until the shrimp turn pink; drain. Peel and devein the shrimp.

◆ Combine the tomatoes, white wine, oil, basil, oregano, red pepper flakes and garlic in a saucepan and mix well.

◆ Cook until of a sauce consistency, stirring frequently.

◆ Stir in the shrimp gently. Spoon into a baking dish; sprinkle with the cheese.

◆ Bake at 400 degrees for 10 minutes.

◆ Spoon the pasta onto a serving platter; top with the shrimp and sauce.

◆ Serve immediately.

◆ Makes 6 to 8 servings.

The Ellicott Square Building was once known as the largest office building in America. The central court of the Ellicott Square Building is based upon Italian art inlays similar to those of the Taj Mahal.

Fillets of Sole Sauté

Serve with fried sweet potatoes and a green vegetable.

1 cup milk

4 eggs

1 cup flour

Salt and pepper to taste

2 cups nuts (almonds,
walnuts, pecans or
cashews or a mixture of
all or your preference)

1 cup butter

8 (2- to 3-ounce) fillets grey
or lemon sole

½ cup bourbon or white
wine plus a small
amount of lemon juice

1 cup whipping cream

2 tablespoons chopped fresh
parsley

◆ Beat the milk and eggs together in a bowl.

◆ Combine the flour, salt and pepper in a bowl.

◆ Grind the nuts in a food processor. Pour into a bowl.

◆ Heat the butter in a heavy ovenproof saucepan or sauté pan until melted.

◆ Dip the fillets in the flour mixture; dip in the egg mixture. Coat with the nuts. Arrange the fillets in the prepared saucepan or sauté pan.

◆ Sauté until the nuts are golden brown and the fillets flake easily. Transfer the fillets to an ovenproof dish. Keep warm in a 300-degree oven.

◆ Discard any pan drippings from the saucepan or sauté pan. Add the bourbon or white wine with lemon.

◆ Cook until heated. Stir in the whipping cream.

◆ Cook until the consistency of a smooth sauce, stirring constantly. Spoon the sauce onto 8 dinner plates; top with the sole. Sprinkle with the parsley.

◆ Makes 8 servings.

Sesame Balsamic Tuna

2 (½-inch) tuna steaks

½ cup balsamic vinegar

¼ cup dark sesame oil

2 tablespoons freshly grated
  gingerroot

2 tablespoons chopped fresh
  cilantro

2 green onions, chopped

4 teaspoons sugar

8 ounces mushrooms, sliced

½ tablespoon sesame oil

————◆————

*Ginger may be purchased
"by the hand" in the
produce department of your
local grocery store. It can be
frozen for future use. No
need to thaw before grating
or slicing. Ginger generally
does not require peeling.*

◆ Rinse the tuna steaks and pat dry.
  Arrange in a shallow dish.

◆ Combine the balsamic vinegar, ¼
  cup sesame oil, gingerroot, cilantro,
  green onions and sugar in a bowl and
  mix well. Pour over the tuna, turning
  to coat.

◆ Marinate, covered, in the refrigerator
  for 1 hour, turning occasionally. Drain,
  reserving the marinade.

◆ Preheat the grill on high for 10
  minutes. Place the tuna steaks on the
  grill rack.

◆ Grill for 3 to 4 minutes per side or
  until the tuna flakes easily.

◆ Sauté the mushrooms in ½ tablespoon
  sesame oil in a skillet until brown on
  both sides. Stir in the reserved
  marinade.

◆ Cook until heated through.

◆ Arrange the tuna steaks on a serving
  platter. Pour the mushroom sauce over
  the steaks.

◆ Makes 2 servings.

Thai Peanut Shrimp and Linguini

1 pound linguini

Salt to taste

1 pound large shrimp

2 to 3 quarts water

½ cup creamy peanut butter

½ cup low-sodium soy sauce

½ cup chicken broth

2 tablespoons honey

1 tablespoon lime juice

2 teaspoons crushed red pepper

1½ teaspoons cornstarch

½ cup chopped scallions

Linguini is narrow flat strands of pasta about one-eighth inch wide.

◆ Cook the linguini in boiling salted water in a saucepan using package directions; drain.

◆ Peel and devein the shrimp.

◆ Bring 2 to 3 quarts water to a boil in a stockpot. Add the shrimp.

◆ Boil for 5 to 7 minutes or until the shrimp turn pink; drain.

◆ Combine the peanut butter, soy sauce, broth, honey, lime juice, red pepper and cornstarch in a saucepan and mix well.

◆ Cook for 5 minutes or until thickened, stirring constantly.

◆ Toss the hot linguini, shrimp, sauce and scallions in a bowl. Spoon onto a serving platter.

◆ Makes 6 servings.

Three brothers in Buffalo started their careers locally by selling peanuts at ball games, and went on to form Sportservice, one of the nation's largest stadium concessionaires.

Rigatoni with Chicken Fennel Mousse

12 ounces rigatoni

1 tablespoon olive oil

12 ounces boneless skinless
    chicken breasts

1 tablespoon fennel seeds,
    chopped

1 egg white

1¼ cups whipping cream

1 teaspoon kosher salt

½ teaspoon white pepper

¼ teaspoon Tabasco sauce

2½ cups whipping cream

½ cup grated Romano
    cheese

1 teaspoon kosher salt

½ teaspoon white pepper

◆ Cook the pasta using package directions until al dente. Drain, rinse with cold water and drain again. Toss the pasta with the olive oil in a bowl.

◆ Rinse the chicken and pat dry. Place the chicken in a food processor container fitted with a steel blade. Pulse 6 to 8 times. Add the fennel seeds and egg white. Process for 2 minutes or until puréed.

◆ Chill the chicken mixture for 5 minutes in a nest of ice water. (To make the nest, fill a bowl ⅓ full with ice and water. Spoon the chicken mixture in a smaller bowl. Nest the smaller bowl in the larger bowl.) Add 1¼ cups whipping cream ¼ cup at a time to the chicken mixture, mixing well after each addition. Stir in 1 teaspoon kosher salt, ½ teaspoon white pepper and Tabasco sauce. Stuff the pasta with the chicken mixture. Arrange in a baking dish. May be prepared to this point, covered and refrigerated or frozen for future use.

◆ Bring 2½ cups whipping cream to a boil in a heavy saucepan. Stir in the cheese, 1 teaspoon kosher salt and ½ teaspoon white pepper. Pour over the stuffed pasta.

◆ Bake at 400 degrees for 30 to 45 minutes or until bubbly. Garnish with chopped fresh chives or chopped fresh Italian parsley.

◆ Makes 4 entrée or 6 appetizer servings.

The Larkin Soap Company was the first to place prizes into its products.

Rotini with Chicken, Gorgonzola Cheese and Peas

16 ounces rotini

4 boneless skinless chicken
    breast halves

4 tablespoons olive oil

1 red onion, sliced

1 cup sliced mushrooms

2 cloves of garlic, chopped

½ cup chicken stock

½ teaspoon pepper

4 ounces Gorgonzola
    cheese, crumbled

½ cup green peas

Salt to taste

◆ Cook the pasta using package directions. Drain and rinse.

◆ Rinse the chicken and pat dry.

◆ Heat 1 tablespoon of the olive oil in a 10-inch skillet over medium-high heat. Add the chicken.

◆ Sauté the chicken in the hot olive oil until cooked through and golden brown on both sides, turning once. Transfer the chicken to a platter; slice. Tent with foil to keep warm.

◆ Add the remaining 3 tablespoons olive oil to the pan drippings and heat.

◆ Add the onion, mushrooms and garlic to the skillet. Sauté until the onion is tender. Return the chicken and any accumulated juices to the skillet.

◆ Cook until heated through, stirring frequently. Add the stock, pepper and pasta and mix well.

◆ Cook for 2 minutes to reduce the liquid, stirring frequently. Add the cheese and peas, tossing to mix. Season with salt. Serve immediately.

◆ Makes 4 servings.

Passion Pasta

12 ounces boneless skinless chicken breasts

¼ cup extra-virgin olive oil

2 cups broccoli florets

¾ cup chicken broth

1 teaspoon basil

½ teaspoon red pepper flakes

Salt and black pepper to taste

2 tablespoons butter or margarine

8 ounces bow tie pasta, cooked, drained

◆ Rinse the chicken and pat dry. Cut into strips.

◆ Sauté the chicken in the olive oil in a large skillet until cooked through; push the chicken to one side of the skillet. Add the broccoli.

◆ Sauté until the broccoli is tender-crisp. Stir in the broth, basil, red pepper flakes, salt and black pepper. Add the butter and mix well.

◆ Simmer, covered, for 5 minutes, stirring occasionally. Remove from heat. Toss with the pasta in a bowl.

◆ Serve immediately with grated Parmesan or Romano cheese if desired.

◆ Makes 4 servings.

Our distinct seasons provide countless recreation and leisure opportunities for residents and visitors. Despite common misconceptions about Buffalo's snowfall, Buffalo's location along Lake Erie makes the climate one of the mildest in the Northeast. Buffalo can also expect more days with temperatures above seventy-five degrees than days with snow on the ground.

Angel Hair Pasta with Shrimp, Asparagus and Fresh Basil

Try this with snow peas, sugar snap peas or broccoli for the asparagus.

15 thin stalks fresh
  asparagus

1 tablespoon olive oil

4 medium cloves of garlic,
  minced

¼ teaspoon ground pepper

6 medium plum tomatoes,
  seeded, chopped

½ cup dry white wine

¼ teaspoon salt

12 ounces peeled cooked
  shrimp

1 tablespoon butter

9 ounces fresh angel hair
  pasta, cooked, drained

¼ cup shredded fresh basil

Angel hair pasta is very thin spaghetti, usually dried separately, but sometimes dried in fifteen to twenty strands and twisted into a cluster.

◆ Trim the asparagus. Rinse in cold water; drain. Remove the tips and reserve. Cut the remaining stalks diagonally into 1-inch pieces.

◆ Heat the olive oil in a large skillet over medium heat. Add the garlic and pepper and mix well.

◆ Cook for 1 minute, stirring constantly. Stir in the tomatoes.

◆ Cook for 2 minutes, stirring frequently. Add the asparagus stalks, white wine and salt and mix well.

◆ Cook for 3 minutes, stirring frequently. Stir in the asparagus tips and shrimp.

◆ Cook for 1 minute, stirring constantly. Add the butter. (Butter is used to bind the sauce. Margarine might not be as effective.)

◆ Cook until the butter melts, stirring constantly. Add the pasta, tossing to mix. Stir in the basil.

◆ Makes 3 servings.

Jambalaya Pasta

8 ounces chicken strips

1 tablespoon vegetable oil

1 pound jumbo Gulf
   shrimp, peeled

8 ounces chorizo or
   andouille sausage,
   cooked, drained

1 cup white wine

12 ounces fettuccini,
   cooked, drained

2 cups chicken stock

1½ cups crushed tomatoes

1 cup whipping cream

2 tablespoons Cajun
   seasoning

1 or 2 green onions, sliced

◆ Rinse the chicken and pat dry.

◆ Brown the chicken on all sides in
   the oil in a 12-inch sauté pan. Add the
   shrimp and sausage.

◆ Sauté lightly. Deglaze the pan with the
   white wine. Stir in the fettuccini, stock,
   tomatoes, whipping cream and Cajun
   seasoning.

◆ Cook until slightly thickened, stirring
   constantly. Add the green onions and
   mix well.

◆ Spoon into individual pasta bowls.

◆ Makes 4 to 6 servings.

A Buffalo church that
has historical significance
is the Macedonian
Baptist Church,
originally known as the
Michigan Avenue
Church. This church was
an important Under-
ground Railroad Station
during the fugitive slave
days preceding the Civil
War (1861–1865) as
slaves were making their
way to Canada.

Seafood Pasta with Peppers and Greek Olives

12 to 16 ounces lemon-pepper pasta

10 ounces medium peeled shrimp

1 bunch green onions, chopped

Vegetable oil

2 tomatoes, chopped

1 green bell pepper, julienned

1 red bell pepper, julienned

¼ cup dry white wine

4 ounces black Greek olives

Chopped fresh parsley and basil to taste

Ground pepper to taste

Grated Parmesan cheese

◆ Cook the pasta using package directions. Drain and rinse.

◆ Stir-fry the shrimp and green onions in oil in a skillet over high heat for 1½ minutes. Add the tomatoes and bell peppers.

◆ Stir-fry until the shrimp turn pink. Add the white wine, olives, parsley, basil and pepper. Spoon over the hot pasta on a serving platter. Sprinkle with Parmesan cheese.

◆ May add additional favorite fresh herbs if desired.

◆ Makes 4 servings.

———◆———

Basil is an annual herb that can be grown indoors or outdoors. Basil should be stored, unwashed, in an airtight container. It is excellent cooked or fresh.

Chinese Pasta

The flavor of this pasta dish is best when prepared just before serving.

8 ounces spaghetti

1 large red bell pepper, chopped

8 ounces mushrooms, sliced

1 bunch green onions with tops, cut into 1-inch pieces

4 ounces snow peas, trimmed

1 tablespoon freshly grated gingerroot

1 tablespoon sherry

1 tablespoon soy sauce

1 tablespoon dark sesame oil

¼ cup chopped fresh cilantro

Freshly ground pepper to taste

Spaghetti is wheat flour pasta dried into long thin strands of pasta.

◆ Cook the pasta using package directions until al dente. Drain and rinse.

◆ Spread the red pepper, mushrooms and green onions in a single layer on a baking sheet.

◆ Roast at 375 degrees until the vegetables are light brown but not soft, turning once.

◆ Steam the snow peas in a steamer for 3 minutes.

◆ Combine the pasta, roasted vegetables and snow peas in a bowl and mix gently. Add a mixture of the gingerroot, sherry, soy sauce and sesame oil, tossing to coat.

◆ Spoon onto a serving platter. Sprinkle with the cilantro and pepper.

◆ Cool the roasted vegetables before tossing with the pasta and dressing for a cold dish.

◆ Makes 4 servings.

Penne with Bacon and Three Cheeses

12 ounces penne

Salt to taste

4 ounces bacon, chopped

¼ cup butter

*½ cup sliced fresh
mushrooms*

1 cup whipping cream

*½ cup shredded Swiss
cheese*

*½ cup shredded Cheddar
cheese*

*¼ cup grated Parmesan
cheese*

⅛ teaspoon nutmeg

Salt and pepper to taste

*Grated Parmesan cheese to
taste*

Chopped fresh parsley

◆ Cook the pasta in boiling salted water in a saucepan until al dente. Drain and rinse. Cover to keep warm.

◆ Sauté the bacon in a nonstick skillet over medium heat until almost crisp. Transfer the bacon with a slotted spoon to a paper towel to drain. Reserve 2 tablespoons of the pan drippings.

◆ Combine the reserved pan drippings and butter in the skillet. Heat until the butter melts. Add the mushrooms and bacon.

◆ Sauté for 3 minutes. Stir in the whipping cream.

◆ Simmer for 3 minutes or until slightly thickened, stirring frequently.

◆ Combine the Swiss cheese, Cheddar cheese and ¼ cup Parmesan cheese in a bowl and mix well. Add the cheese mixture ¼ cup at a time to the cream mixture, stirring constantly after each addition until the cheese melts. Stir in the nutmeg, salt and pepper. Add the pasta, tossing to coat.

◆ Spoon into individual pasta bowls. Sprinkle with Parmesan cheese to taste and parsley.

◆ Makes 3 to 4 servings.

Penne with Mushrooms, Tomatoes and Gorgonzola Cheese

2 tablespoons olive oil

6 ounces fresh mushrooms, sliced

½ teaspoon basil

½ teaspoon thyme

½ teaspoon oregano

¼ teaspoon crushed red pepper

1 large tomato, chopped

6 tablespoons chicken stock

1 teaspoon chopped fresh garlic

2 teaspoons chopped fresh parsley

Salt and pepper to taste

8 ounces penne, cooked, drained

6 ounces Gorgonzola cheese, crumbled

◆ Heat the olive oil in a 10-inch sauté pan over medium-high heat. Add the mushrooms, basil, thyme, oregano and red pepper and mix well.

◆ Sauté until the mushrooms are tender. Stir in the tomato.

◆ Sauté for 1 minute. Add the stock and garlic and mix well.

◆ Simmer for 1 minute. Stir in the parsley; season with salt and pepper.

◆ Combine the mushroom mixture with the hot pasta in a bowl, tossing to mix. Spoon onto a serving platter. Sprinkle with the Gorgonzola cheese. Serve immediately.

◆ Makes 2 servings.

When cooking pasta, use plenty of boiling water with a little vegetable oil and a generous pinch of salt. Cook until the pasta is tender but still firm to the bite, or al dente. Drain quickly and add a small quantity of butter or vegetable oil before serving.

Linguini with Roasted Yellow Pepper Sauce

3 yellow bell peppers

Vegetable oil

¾ cup extra-virgin olive oil

1 hard-cooked egg yolk

1 clove of garlic

Salt and pepper to taste

*1½ pounds linguini,
    cooked, drained*

*5 teaspoons chopped fresh
    parsley*

---

*May substitute ⅛ teaspoon
garlic powder, ⅛ teaspoon
instant minced garlic, ¾
teaspoon garlic salt, or 5
drops of liquid garlic for 1
fresh clove of garlic.*

◆ Rub the yellow peppers with vegetable oil. Place on a grill rack.

◆ Grill over hot coals until the skin is blistered and charred on all sides, turning frequently. Place in a sealable plastic bag.

◆ Steam until cool. Peel and seed the yellow peppers; cut into large pieces.

◆ Combine the yellow peppers, ¾ cup olive oil, egg yolk and garlic in a food processor container.

◆ Process until smooth. Season with salt and pepper. Spoon into a saucepan.

◆ Cook until heated through, stirring frequently. Pour over the hot pasta in a bowl, tossing to mix. Spoon onto a serving platter. Sprinkle with the parsley.

◆ Makes 6 servings.

Pasta with Vodka

1 pound ziti

6 tablespoons butter

2 cloves of garlic, minced

1 teaspoon crushed red
    pepper flakes

1 cup vodka

1 cup crushed tomatoes

1 cup whipping cream

1 teaspoon salt

1 cup grated Parmesan
    cheese

Pepper to taste

---

*Serve with Feta-Tomato
Bread. Prepare by slicing
1 loaf Italian bread lengthwise into halves. Spread
the cut sides with butter.
Place on a baking sheet.
Bake until the butter melts.
Top each half with sliced
tomatoes; sprinkle with
feta cheese.*

◆ Cook the pasta in boiling water in
    a saucepan until al dente. Drain
    and rinse.

◆ Heat the butter in a saucepan until
    melted. Add the garlic and red
    pepper flakes.

◆ Sauté for 2 minutes. Stir in the vodka.

◆ Simmer for 5 minutes, stirring
    occasionally. Add the tomatoes and
    mix well.

◆ Simmer for 5 minutes, stirring
    occasionally. Stir in the whipping
    cream and salt.

◆ Simmer for 10 minutes, stirring
    frequently. Add the cheese and mix
    well. Add pepper to taste. Pour over
    the pasta in a bowl, tossing to mix.
    Serve immediately.

◆ Makes 4 servings.

Greek-Style Pasta and Phyllo

10 to 12 phyllo sheets

16 ounces macaroni or favorite pasta, cooked, drained

½ cup butter, softened

2 cups crumbled feta cheese

2 cups grated Parmesan cheese

1½ cups ricotta cheese

4 eggs, beaten

2 cups milk

Salt and pepper to taste

Melted butter

◆ Thaw the pastry using package directions.

◆ Toss the warm pasta with ½ cup butter in a bowl. Add a mixture of the feta cheese, Parmesan cheese and ricotta cheese, stirring to mix.

◆ Whisk the eggs, milk, salt and pepper together. Add to the pasta mixture. Spoon into a 9x12-inch baking dish. Top with the phyllo 1 sheet at a time, drizzling each sheet with melted butter. Score the top with a razor blade or sharp knife.

◆ Bake at 350 degrees for 45 minutes or until brown. Serve hot or cold.

◆ Makes 6 to 8 servings.

Ultimate Pesto

2 cups fresh basil

¾ cup grated Parmesan cheese

6 tablespoons olive oil

¼ cup fresh Italian parsley

3 tablespoons butter

2 tablespoons walnuts

1 tablespoon pine nuts

4 to 5 cloves of garlic

¼ teaspoon pepper

⅛ teaspoon nutmeg

⅛ teaspoon grated orange peel

◆ Combine the basil, cheese, olive oil, parsley, butter, walnuts, pine nuts, garlic, pepper, nutmeg and orange peel in a food processor container.

◆ Process until of the desired consistency.

◆ Toss the pesto with hot cooked pasta of your choice or spread on slices of French bread.

◆ Makes 6 to 8 servings.

Delectable DESSERTS

On the Avenue

22" x 30"   Corporate Collection

"The spirit is warm and glowing. I really enjoy seeing and painting the vitality of architecture in this area. I find that the more I paint it, the more there is to see and to translate—beautiful and elegant!"   M.M.M.

The Buffalo Club was the city's first social club and is one of the twenty-five oldest clubs in the United States. The Club's Certificate of Incorporation was drafted on December 26, 1866 by such prominent citizens as Millard Fillmore, William Fargo (founder of Wells-Fargo), Isaac Verplanck (Justice of the Superior Court), William Dorsheimer (Lieutenant Governor of the State of New York), Delevan Clark, and Josiah Jewett. The incorporation was approved January 2, 1867. The objective was to "promote" social interaction amongst its members.

Winter Farmscape
22" x 30"   Corporate Collection

*"Painting is a long process of searching and wandering
with exuberance, frustration, analysis, and quiet looking.
Painting is about bigness. The linking of white areas helps
to organize the whole presentation. Nature gives us so much
artistry and vitality. We need to be ready to receive." MMM*

Many of Western New York's southern suburbs receive an
average lake effect snowfall of 150 inches—considerably
more than downtown Buffalo, which receives only about 74 inches
each year. These snowfalls transform the Southtowns into a skiers'
paradise, with twenty ski areas located within a two-hour drive
from downtown Buffalo.

Ransom House

22" x 30"   Corporate Collection

"There is mystery. It is a timeless era. I am attracted to the afternoon February sunlight. Light creates color and color triggers a response."   MMM

In 1883, a prominent Buffalo lumber family, the Bemises, built their private residence at 267 North Street. From the Pan-American Exposition, which was held in Buffalo in 1901, the owners purchased an entire display room and incorporated it into the second floor of their home. To this day, the room has been preserved. In 1983 the house, owned by the Ransom Family, was selected for Junior League of Buffalo's and *The Buffalo News'* second Decorators' Show House. The proceeds from this Show House were used for a project on the Downtown Transit Mall. In 1995, Ransom House was renovated and is currently used as office space.

Delectable
DESSERTS

Apple Rum Cake

A wonderful aroma fills your house when this delicious cake is being baked.

¾ cup dark rum

4 cups chopped peeled
   apples

2 cups flour

2 teaspoons baking soda

2 teaspoons apple pie spice
   or cinnamon

1 teaspoon salt

2 cups sugar

1 cup vegetable oil

2 eggs, beaten

1 cup raisins

◆ Pour the rum over the apples in a bowl, tossing to mix.

◆ Sift the flour, baking soda, apple pie spice and salt together.

◆ Beat the sugar, oil and eggs in a mixer bowl until blended. Stir in half the dry ingredients.

◆ Stir the raisins into the apple mixture. Add the remaining dry ingredients and mix well. Stir into the egg mixture. Spoon into a 9x13-inch cake pan.

◆ Bake at 350 degrees for 1¼ hours. Cool in the pan on a wire rack.

◆ Serve with vanilla ice cream or whipped cream.

◆ Makes 16 servings.

Buffalo musicians formed the first black union in Buffalo on February 3, 1917.

Blueberry Crumb Cake

1 pint blueberries

½ teaspoon lemon zest

2¼ cups flour

¾ cup sugar

¾ cup margarine

1 teaspoon baking soda

½ cup plain low-fat yogurt

1 egg, lightly beaten

1 teaspoon lemon juice

In many recipes 1 cup granulated sugar can be replaced by 1 cup of corn syrup, molasses, or honey, reducing the amount of liquid in the recipe by 2 to 4 tablespoons or by using 1 cup packed brown sugar

◆ Toss the blueberries gently with the lemon zest in a bowl.

◆ Combine 2 cups of the flour and sugar in a bowl. Cut in the margarine until crumbly. Reserve 1½ cups of the crumb mixture for the topping.

◆ Stir a mixture of the remaining ¼ cup flour and baking soda into the remaining crumb mixture until mixed.

◆ Add the yogurt, egg and lemon juice and mix well. Fold in 1 cup of the blueberries.

◆ Spread the batter in a lightly buttered 10-inch springform pan. Sprinkle with the remaining blueberries.

◆ Top with the reserved crumb mixture. Place the springform pan on a baking sheet.

◆ Bake at 400 degrees for 1 hour or until light brown and the cake tests done.

◆ Makes 16 servings.

Elan's frozen yogurt was first sold in the Western New York region in 1986.

Carrot Cake

2 cups sifted flour

2 teaspoons baking powder

2 teaspoons cinnamon

1½ teaspoons baking soda

1½ teaspoons salt

2 cups sugar

1½ cups safflower oil

4 eggs

2 cups finely grated carrots

1 (8-ounce) can crushed pineapple, drained

1 (4-ounce) package flaked coconut

½ cup chopped walnuts or pecans

Rich Cream Cheese Frosting (below)

◆ Sift the flour, baking powder, cinnamon, baking soda and salt into a bowl and mix well. Add the sugar, safflower oil and eggs and mix well. Stir in the carrots, pineapple, coconut and walnuts. Spoon into 3 greased and floured or waxed-paper-lined 9-inch round cake pans.

◆ Bake at 350 degrees for 35 to 40 minutes or until the layers test done.

◆ Cool slightly in the pans on a wire rack. Invert onto a wire rack to cool completely.

◆ Spread the Cream Cheese Frosting between the layers and over the top and side of the cake. Arrange walnut or pecan halves in a decorative manner around the outer edge of the cake if desired.

◆ Makes 12 servings.

Rich Cream Cheese Frosting

8 ounces cream cheese, softened

½ cup butter or margarine, softened

1 teaspoon vanilla extract

1 (1-pound) package confectioners' sugar

Milk

◆ Beat the cream cheese, butter and vanilla in a mixer bowl until creamy, scraping the bowl occasionally. Add the confectioners' sugar gradually, beating constantly until blended. Beat in just enough milk to make of a spreading consistency.

◆ Makes 12 servings.

Bittersweet Chocolate Cake with Raspberry Cream

Sugar to taste

1 cup butter

*6 ounces semisweet
chocolate, chopped*

*4 ounces unsweetened
chocolate, chopped*

1¼ cups sugar

4 extra-large eggs

1 tablespoon flour

Raspberry Cream (below)

◆ Butter the bottom and side of a 9-inch springform pan; sprinkle with sugar. Tap out excess sugar. Wrap the outer bottom and 2 inches up the side of the springform pan with foil.

◆ Combine 1 cup butter and chocolate in a double boiler. Cook over simmering water until blended, stirring frequently. Remove from water.

◆ Whisk the sugar and eggs together in a bowl. Stir in the flour. Add the chocolate mixture and mix well. Spoon into the prepared pan. Place the springform pan in a larger baking pan. Add boiling water to reach ½ inch up the side of the pan.

◆ Bake at 325 degrees for 1 hour or until the top is firm and a wooden pick inserted in the middle comes out with some moist crumbs attached. Remove the springform pan to a wire rack to cool completely.

◆ Place on a serving platter; remove side. Slice and serve with Raspberry Cream.

◆ Makes 10 servings.

Raspberry Cream

1 cup whipping cream

*3 tablespoons confectioners'
sugar*

½ cup raspberries

◆ Beat the whipping cream, confectioners' sugar and raspberries in a mixer bowl until soft peaks form, scraping the bowl occasionally.

◆ Makes 10 servings.

*North Tonawanda,
a suburb of Buffalo, is
the home of a 1916
antique carrousel.*

Rhubarb Cake

2 cups flour

1 teaspoon baking soda

1½ cups sugar

½ cup margarine, softened

1 teaspoon vanilla extract

½ teaspoon salt

2 eggs

1 cup buttermilk

2 cups thinly sliced rhubarb

½ cup sugar

1½ teaspoons cinnamon

———◆———

*All-purpose flour is a blend
of hard and soft wheats.
Enriched all-purpose flours
have been enriched with B
vitamins and iron.*

♦ Sift the flour and baking soda together.

♦ Beat 1½ cups sugar, margarine, vanilla and salt in a mixer bowl until creamy, scraping the bowl occasionally. Add the eggs.

♦ Beat until fluffy. Add the flour mixture and buttermilk alternately, mixing well after each addition. Stir in the rhubarb. Spoon into a lightly greased and floured 9x13-inch cake pan.

♦ Combine ½ cup sugar and cinnamon in a bowl and mix well. Sprinkle over the prepared layer.

♦ Bake at 350 degrees for 45 minutes or until the cake tests done. Serve with whipped cream.

♦ Makes 15 servings.

Chocolate Toffee Frosting

2 cups whipping cream

1 cup confectioners' sugar

¼ cup baking cocoa

6 toffee candy bars, crushed

♦ Mix the whipping cream, confectioners' sugar and baking cocoa in a bowl. Chill, covered, for 8 to 10 hours.

♦ Beat the whipping cream mixture in a mixer bowl until peaks form. Fold in the crushed candy bars.

♦ Use to frost an angel food cake, German chocolate cake, chocolate cake, yellow cake or white cake. May double the recipe.

♦ Makes frosting for one 3-layer cake.

Millie's Truffles

½ cup unsalted butter

4 ounces milk chocolate

4 ounces semisweet chocolate

2 tablespoons confectioners' sugar

3 egg yolks, beaten

2 tablespoons Grand Marnier or other liqueur

Baking cocoa

◆ Combine the butter, milk chocolate and semisweet chocolate in a double boiler.

◆ Cook until blended, stirring frequently. Stir in the confectioners' sugar. Stir a small amount of the hot mixture into the egg yolks; stir the egg yolks gradually into the hot mixture. Stir in the liqueur. Spoon into a nonmetal dish.

◆ Chill, covered, for 12 to 24 hours.

◆ Shape into 1-inch balls; roll the truffles in baking cocoa.

◆ Makes 1½ dozen.

Swedish Pecans

Great holiday treat! Place the pecans in decorative cellophane bags, tie with ribbons, and give to family and friends for holiday gifts.

½ cup butter

2 egg whites

1 cup sugar

1 pound pecan halves

◆ Heat the butter in a baking pan until melted.

◆ Beat the egg whites in a mixer bowl until frothy. Add the sugar, beating until blended. Add the pecans, stirring until coated. Spread in the prepared pan.

◆ Bake at 275 to 300 degrees for 45 minutes, stirring every 10 to 15 minutes. Spread on parchment paper to cool.

◆ Makes 8 to 10 servings.

The Erie County Fair, which originated in the 1820s, is currently the second-largest county fair in the United States.

Youngstown

Thirty-some miles from Buffalo, located just below the Falls on the mouth of the Niagara River as it opens into Lake Ontario, lies the little sleepy village of Youngstown, New York. Every year during the last weekend of July the town comes to life in its own inimitable way. The Youngstown Yacht Club hosts the Level Regatta, initiated in 1973 by club member and local sailor Don Finkle. ➤

Addictive Youngstown Chips

4½ cups flour

2 teaspoons baking powder

2 teaspoons baking soda

1 teaspoon salt

2 cups melted unsalted butter

2 cups sugar

2 cups packed brown sugar

4 eggs, at room temperature

2 teaspoons vanilla extract

2 cups rolled oats

2 cups cornflakes

2 cups chocolate chips

2 cups chopped pecans

1 cup shredded coconut or dried cranberries

◆ Sift the flour, baking powder, baking soda and salt together.

◆ Beat the butter, sugar, brown sugar, eggs and vanilla in a mixer bowl until blended. Stir in the flour mixture.

◆ Add the oats, cornflakes, chocolate chips, pecans and coconut 1 at a time, mixing well after each addition.

◆ Drop by ¼ cupfuls 2 inches apart onto an ungreased cookie sheet.

◆ Bake at 350 degrees for 10 to 14 minutes or until light brown around the edges. Remove to a wire rack to cool.

◆ Makes 20 cookies.

Chocolate Lace Cookies

1 cup quick-cooking oats

1 cup sugar

½ teaspoon salt

½ cup melted margarine

1 egg

1 teaspoon vanilla extract

1 teaspoon orange juice

1 cup semisweet chocolate
  chips

◆ Combine the oats, sugar and salt in a bowl and mix well. Stir in the margarine, egg, vanilla and orange juice. Drop by ½ teaspoonfuls onto foil-lined cookie sheets.

◆ Bake at 350 degrees for 6 to 11 minutes or until the edges are brown and slightly tan in the center. Remove foil with cookies to wire rack to cool. Peel off the foil when cool.

◆ Heat the chocolate chips in a double boiler over simmering water until melted. Spread the melted chocolate over 1 side of half the cookies. Top with the remaining cookies to form sandwiches.

◆ Makes 3 dozen cookies.

The race was first called Ton Level because the first thirteen boats to participate were classified by weight. Now the largest regatta of its kind in the nation, the gathering draws close to five hundred boats in nearly fifty classes to race on five courses. The yachts come from as far away as Montreal. The weekend festivities include a variety of bands, summer fare, and, of course, coveted trophies for each class.

Chocolate Oatmeal Bars

3 cups rolled oats

2½ cups sifted flour

2 cups packed brown sugar

1 cup margarine

2 eggs, beaten

2 teaspoons vanilla extract

1 teaspoon baking soda

1 teaspoon salt

2 cups chocolate chips

1 (14-ounce) can sweetened
   condensed milk

1½ cups chopped walnuts

2 tablespoons butter

2 teaspoons vanilla extract

½ teaspoon salt

◆ Combine the oats, flour, brown sugar, margarine, eggs, 2 teaspoons vanilla, baking soda and 1 teaspoon salt in a double boiler.

◆ Heat until mixed, stirring frequently. Reserve half the mixture. Pat the remaining mixture over the bottom of a baking pan.

◆ Combine the chocolate chips, condensed milk, walnuts, butter, 2 teaspoons vanilla and ½ teaspoon salt in a double boiler.

◆ Heat until mixed, stirring frequently. Spread over the prepared layer. Top with the reserved oat mixture.

◆ Bake at 350 degrees for 25 minutes.

◆ Let stand until cool. Cut into bars. Store in an airtight container.

◆ Makes 3 to 4 dozen bars.

Esther Cleveland,
daughter of president and
former Buffalonian
Grover Cleveland, was
the first child to be born in
the White House.

Fruitcake Cookies

2½ cups flour

1 teaspoon baking soda

1 teaspoon salt

1 teaspoon cinnamon

1½ cups sugar

1 cup margarine, softened

2 eggs

32 ounces pitted dates,
   coarsely chopped

1 (8-ounce) package
   candied pineapple
   chunks

1 cup candied cherries

4 ounces almonds or
   walnuts, chopped

1 cup chopped Brazil nuts

One pound unshelled nuts
equals one cup chopped
shelled nuts.

◆ Sift the flour, baking soda, salt and
  cinnamon together.

◆ Beat the sugar, margarine and eggs in
  a mixer bowl until light and fluffy,
  scraping the bowl occasionally. Stir in
  the flour mixture until blended. Add
  the dates, pineapple, cherries, almonds
  and Brazil nuts and mix well.

◆ Drop by level tablespoonfuls 2 inches
  apart onto an ungreased cookie sheet.

◆ Bake at 400 degrees for 8 to 10
  minutes or until light brown around
  the edges.

◆ Cool on the cookie sheet for 1 minute.
  Remove to a wire rack to cool
  completely.

◆ Makes 8 dozen cookies.

Orange Almond Biscotti

3¼ cups flour

1 tablespoon baking powder

¾ cup sugar

½ cup butter, softened

5 eggs

2 tablespoons grated orange peel

1 tablespoon vanilla extract

⅔ cup chopped almonds

◆ Combine the flour and baking powder in a bowl and mix well.

◆ Beat the sugar and butter in a mixer bowl until pale yellow, scraping the bowl occasionally. Beat in the eggs, orange peel and vanilla until mixed. Add the flour mixture, beating until mixed; the dough will be sticky. Stir in the almonds.

◆ Divide the dough into 3 equal portions. Wrap each portion in plastic wrap.

◆ Chill for 3 hours or until firm. Shape each portion into a 12-inch log on a lightly floured surface. Arrange the logs 3 inches apart on 2 greased cookie sheets.

◆ Bake at 350 degrees for 30 to 35 minutes or until firm in the center and slightly cracked on top.

◆ Cool on the cookie sheets on a wire rack for 10 minutes. Transfer the logs carefully to a cutting board. Cut each log diagonally into 15 slices using a serrated knife. Arrange the slices cut side down on a cookie sheet.

◆ Bake for 12 to 15 minutes or until the cookies are dry and light brown, turning once. Remove to a wire rack to cool completely.

◆ Makes 45 cookies.

Pumpkin Bars

1 cup flour

1 cup packed brown sugar

¾ cup canned pumpkin

½ cup butter, softened

2 eggs

1 teaspoon vanilla extract

½ teaspoon baking soda

½ teaspoon salt

½ teaspoon cinnamon

½ teaspoon nutmeg

½ teaspoon ground cloves

Cream Cheese Frosting
(below)

◆ Combine the flour, brown sugar, pumpkin, butter, eggs, vanilla, baking soda, salt, cinnamon, nutmeg and cloves in a bowl and mix well. Spoon into a 9x13-inch baking pan.

◆ Bake at 350 degrees for 20 minutes.

◆ Let stand until cool. Spread with Cream Cheese Frosting. Cut into bars.

◆ Makes 36 bars.

Cream Cheese Frosting

1 (1-pound) package
   confectioners' sugar

¼ cup butter, softened

3 ounces cream cheese,
   softened

½ teaspoon vanilla extract

Milk

◆ Combine the confectioners' sugar, butter, cream cheese and vanilla in a mixer bowl.

◆ Beat until blended, scraping the bowl occasionally. Add enough milk to bring frosting to desired consistency, beating constantly.

◆ Makes 3 to 4 cups.

Perry's Ice Cream, Inc.

In 1932 Alden School asked an area dairy owner, H. Morton Perry, to provide the school with ice cream (the school dietitian knew that Mr. Perry's mother had a good recipe for ice cream). Mr. Perry prepared the ice cream in his home and The Perry's Ice Cream Company was born.

H. Morton Perry's philosophy—"If my name is on it, I want it to be the best."—is still followed today. That is probably the reason that more than ten million gallons of Perry's Ice Cream is consumed each year.

Harvest Cream Apple Pie

¾ cup sugar

2 tablespoons flour

1 cup sour cream

1 egg

1 teaspoon vanilla extract

¼ teaspoon nutmeg

3 or 4 apples, peeled, sliced

1 unbaked (9-inch) pie shell

½ cup flour

½ cup sugar

1 teaspoon cinnamon

⅓ cup butter, softened

◆ Combine ¾ cup sugar and 2 tablespoons flour in a bowl and mix well. Stir in the sour cream, egg, vanilla and nutmeg. Add the apples and mix gently. Spoon into the pie shell.

◆ Bake at 375 degrees for 45 minutes.

◆ Combine ½ cup flour, ½ cup sugar and cinnamon in a bowl and mix well. Cut in the butter until crumbly. Sprinkle over the baked pie.

◆ Bake at 400 degrees for 10 minutes longer.

◆ Serve warm or at room temperature with vanilla ice cream.

◆ Makes 8 to 10 servings.

One cup sliced or chopped apple is the equivalent of one medium apple.

Fresh Blueberry Tart

1 cup flour

2 tablespoons sugar

½ teaspoon salt

½ cup butter, softened

1 tablespoon white vinegar

3½ to 4 cups fresh
  blueberries

⅔ cup sugar

2 tablespoons flour

¼ teaspoon cinnamon

1 tablespoon lemon juice

2 cups fresh blueberries

◆ Combine 1 cup flour, 2 tablespoons sugar and salt in a bowl and mix well. Cut in the butter until crumbly. Sprinkle with the vinegar.

◆ Knead with floured hands until the mixture clings together. Pat over the bottom and 1 inch up the side of a 9-inch springform pan.

◆ Toss 3½ to 4 cups blueberries, ⅔ cup sugar, 2 tablespoons flour and ¼ teaspoon cinnamon in a bowl gently. Sprinkle with the lemon juice, tossing to coat. Spoon into the prepared pan.

◆ Place the springform pan on the lowest oven rack.

◆ Bake at 375 degrees for 50 minutes. Sprinkle with 2 cups blueberries.

◆ Let stand until cool. Store, covered, in the refrigerator until serving time.

◆ Makes 12 servings.

Rich Products

While traveling from Buffalo to New York City for a supermarket trade show, Robert Rich Sr. packed his supply of non-dairy whip topping with dry ice to keep it fresh. When he arrived, the topping was completely frozen, much to his dismay. Mr. Rich decided to thaw his product and see if it would still whip. It did! To a large degree this product, Rich's Whip Topping, was the catalyst for making Rich Products into the company it is today— the largest privately held frozen food manufacturer in the country.

Quaker Bonnet Lemon Angel Pies

6 egg whites, at room
   temperature

1½ cups superfine sugar

1 cup egg yolks

½ cup sugar

½ cup lemon juice

1 teaspoon lemon zest

1 cup whipped cream

♦ Beat the egg whites in a mixer bowl
until soft peaks form. Add 1½ cups
superfine sugar gradually, beating
constantly until stiff and glossy. Do
not overbeat the meringue or it will
break down.

♦ Pipe the meringue into individual nests
on a parchment-paper-lined baking
sheet or on a parchment-paper-lined
baking sheet sprayed with nonstick
cooking spray.

♦ Bake at 150 to 175 degrees for 3
hours. Leave the oven door open if
you are not able to set the oven
that low. The shells may be baked at
150 degrees for as much as 12 hours to
be sure the shells are completely dry.

♦ Combine the egg yolks, ½ cup sugar,
lemon juice and lemon zest in a
double boiler.

♦ Cook until the mixture holds a ribbon
for 3 seconds when the whisk is lifted
from the mixture, whisking constantly.

♦ Let stand until cool.

♦ Spoon into the meringue nests.

♦ Spread with the whipped cream.

♦ Makes 6 to 8 servings.

Pecan Tarts

2 eggs

1½ cups packed brown
  sugar

2 tablespoons melted butter

½ teaspoon vanilla extract

⅛ teaspoon salt

1 cup chopped pecans

Cream Cheese Pastry
  (below)

◆ Beat the eggs in a bowl. Add the brown sugar, melted butter, vanilla and salt and blend well. Stir in the pecans.

◆ Fill each Cream Cheese Pastry ½ full.

◆ Bake at 350 degrees for 30 minutes.

◆ Makes 48 tarts.

Cream Cheese Pastry

2 cups flour

1 cup butter, softened

6 ounces cream cheese,
  softened

◆ Place the flour in a bowl. Cut in the softened butter and cream cheese until crumbly.

◆ Press 1 tablespoon of the dough into each of 48 miniature muffin cups.

◆ Makes enough pastry for 48 tarts.

Grover Cleveland used the slogan, "Public office is a public trust" when he ran for Mayor of Buffalo.

Pear and Ginger Brown Butter Tart

1½ cups pastry flour

¼ cup sugar

9 tablespoons cold unsalted butter

1 egg

8 hard pears, peeled, cut into halves

4 cups water

6 ounces fresh gingerroot, peeled, cut into ¼-inch slices

⅓ cup lemon juice

1 vanilla bean, split, scraped

Ginger Brown Butter (page 147)

Pear Sauce (page 147)

Ginger Crème Anglaise (page 148)

◆ Mix the flour and sugar in a bowl. Cut in the butter until crumbly. Add 1 egg, stirring just until the dough begins to adhere and forms a ball. Wrap in waxed paper.

◆ Chill for 30 minutes or longer. Roll to fit a 10-inch tart pan on a lightly floured surface. Fit the pastry into a tart pan; trim the edges. Chill in the refrigerator.

◆ Combine the water, gingerroot, lemon juice and vanilla bean in a large saucepan. Add the pears. Poach for 30 to 45 minutes or until tender but firm.

◆ Cool the pears in the liquid. Strain, reserving the poaching liquid and 4 pear halves for the Pear Sauce. Discard the gingerroot and vanilla bean.

◆ Cut 4 of the remaining poached pear halves into thin slices. Arrange over the bottom of the prepared tart pan. Top with the Ginger Brown Butter.

◆ Cut the remaining 8 poached pear halves horizontally into ⅛-inch slices, cutting to but not through the surface; fan slightly. Arrange 7 of the sliced halves over the prepared layers to resemble the spokes of a wheel; place the remaining half in the center.

◆ Bake at 350 degrees for 45 to 60 minutes or until brown and firm.

◆ Let stand until cool. Invert onto a platter. Serve at room temperature with Pear Sauce and Ginger Crème Anglaise.

◆ Makes 8 to 10 servings.

Ginger Brown Butter

7 tablespoons flour

1½ teaspoons ground
    ginger

⅔ cup sugar

2 eggs

½ cup unsalted butter

1½ ounces gingerroot,
    peeled, cut into ¼-inch
    slices, scraped

½ vanilla bean, split,
    scraped

◆ Sift the flour and ground ginger into a
bowl and mix well.

◆ Whisk the sugar and eggs in a bowl
until blended. Add the flour mixture,
stirring until blended.

◆ Heat the butter with the gingerroot and
vanilla bean scrapings in a saucepan
over high heat until brown and foamy,
stirring frequently.

◆ Continue cooking until dark brown
and smoking; mixture will have a nutty
aroma. Add to the egg mixture,
whisking constantly until mixed.

◆ Strain, discarding the gingerroot and
vanilla bean scrapings.

◆ Makes 1 cup.

Pear Sauce

4 poached pear halves

¼ cup lemon juice

3 tablespoons (about) pear
    poaching liquid

◆ Process the pear halves, lemon juice
and poaching liquid in a food
processor or blender until puréed.

◆ Add additional poaching liquid as
needed for a thinner consistency.

◆ Chill, covered, in the refrigerator until
serving time.

◆ Makes 1 cup.

➤

Ginger Crème Anglaise

3 ounces gingerroot, peeled,
cut into ¼-inch slices

2 cups whipping cream

4 egg yolks

3 tablespoons sugar

---

*Add ground, dried, fresh or
frozen gingerroot to desserts
or oriental-style dishes for a
sweet pungent flavor.*

◆ Blanch the gingerroot in boiling
water to cover in a saucepan for 30
seconds; drain.

◆ Heat the gingerroot and whipping
cream in a saucepan until scalded.
Remove from heat.

◆ Let stand, covered, for 30 minutes.
Strain, discarding the gingerroot.

◆ Beat the egg yolks and sugar in a
mixer bowl until blended.

◆ Reheat the cream mixture. Add to
the egg mixture gradually, whisking
constantly until blended. Pour into
the saucepan.

◆ Cook over low heat until thickened,
stirring constantly. Strain into a bowl;
whisk to release heat.

◆ Chill, covered, until serving time.

◆ Makes 2 cups.

*O-Cel-O sponges, a
division of General
Mills, are produced in
the town of Tonawanda,
a suburb of Buffalo.*

Frozen Peanut Butter Pies

1½ cups confectioners' sugar

8 ounces cream cheese, softened

¾ cup crunchy peanut butter

¾ cup milk

12 ounces whipped topping

¼ cup chopped Spanish peanuts

2 baked (8-inch) pie shells

Chocolate curls

◆ Beat the confectioners' sugar and cream cheese in a mixer bowl until fluffy, scraping the bowl occasionally. Add the peanut butter.

◆ Beat until mixed. Add the milk gradually, beating constantly until mixed. Fold in the whipped topping and peanuts.

◆ Spoon into the pie shells.

◆ Freeze for 15 to 30 minutes. Cut into slices. Top each slice with chocolate curls.

◆ Makes 12 to 16 servings.

Prepare chocolate curls by pouring melted chocolate evenly onto a waxed-paper-lined baking sheet. Spread the chocolate into a two- to three-inch strip. Let stand until the chocolate is cool and slightly sticky but not firm. Pull a vegetable peeler or knife slowly across the chocolate until a curl forms, allowing the chocolate to curl on top of the utensil. Transfer the curl with a wooden pick to a plate. Repeat the process with the remaining chocolate. Chill until just before serving.

Allentown

Allentown, a section of the city of Buffalo, is the largest historic preservation district in the United States. Among other distinctions, Allentown was home to two of the country's most notable writers, F. Scott Fitzgerald and Mark Twain.

F. Scott Fitzgerald lived at 29 Irving Place for a short time as a child.

Mark Twain lived on Delaware Avenue while he was editor of the city newspaper The Express. His home is today the location of Business First, a weekly news magazine for Western New York, but is probably better remembered as The Cloister restaurant.

Allentown Clafouti

A great addition to a Sunday brunch.

3 eggs

1¼ cups milk

1 cup plus 2 tablespoons flour

⅓ cup sugar

2 teaspoons vanilla extract

¼ teaspoon nutmeg

¾ cup sliced fresh peaches

¾ cup fresh blueberries

♦ Butter the bottom and side of a 9-inch quiche pan or pie plate.

♦ Beat the eggs in a mixer bowl until foamy. Add the milk, flour, sugar, vanilla and nutmeg.

♦ Beat at low speed until smooth, scraping the bowl occasionally. Spoon into the prepared pan. Top with the peaches and blueberries.

♦ Bake at 350 degrees for 40 to 45 minutes or until a knife inserted in the center comes out clean.

♦ Let stand for 15 minutes before serving.

♦ Makes 6 servings.

Apple Crisp with Lemon Honey Cream

6 ounces dried tart cherries

⅓ cup Calvados

10 large green tart apples, peeled, cut into medium slices

2 tablespoons lemon juice

1½ cups pastry flour

¾ cup sugar

¾ cup packed dark brown sugar

¾ cup cold unsalted butter, cut into small pieces

1 cup walnuts, toasted, coarsely chopped

Lemon Honey Cream (below)

◆ Soak the cherries in the Calvados in a bowl for 30 minutes.

◆ Toss the apple slices with the lemon juice in a bowl. Add the undrained cherries and mix gently. Press the mixture lightly into a 2½-quart shallow baking dish.

◆ Combine the flour, sugar and brown sugar in a bowl and mix well. Cut in the butter just until crumbly. Stir in the walnuts. Sprinkle over the prepared layer.

◆ Bake on the middle oven rack at 375 degrees for 40 minutes or until the apples are tender and brown.

◆ Serve warm with Lemon Honey Cream or vanilla ice cream.

◆ Makes 10 to 12 servings.

Lemon Honey Cream

1 cup whipping cream

2 tablespoons honey

2 teaspoons fresh lemon juice

◆ Combine the whipping cream, honey and lemon juice in a mixer bowl.

◆ Beat at medium speed until thick but not stiff, scraping the bowl occasionally.

◆ Makes 10 to 12 servings.

Each June Buffalo plays host to one of the largest art festivals in the country, the Allentown Art Festival. Begun in 1958, the festival was the brainchild of local businessmen, who wanted to promote area artists and craftsmen as well as provide the community with a delightful way to spend a spring afternoon. Today over 500,000 people attend this weekend event, which celebrates the work of 400 to 450 artists selected from over 1,200 applicants each year.

Apple Cheese Torte

1 cup butter or margarine, softened

⅔ cup sugar

2 cups flour

½ teaspoon vanilla extract

8 ounces cream cheese, softened

¼ cup sugar

1 egg

1 teaspoon vanilla extract

5 or 6 apples, sliced

2 teaspoons lemon juice

⅓ cup sugar

2 teaspoons flour

1 teaspoon cinnamon

¼ cup slivered almonds

◆ Beat the butter and ⅔ cup sugar in a mixer bowl until creamy, scraping the bowl occasionally. Add 2 cups flour and ½ teaspoon vanilla, beating until blended. May add additional flour if needed for desired consistency. Press over the bottom of an 11-inch spring-form pan.

◆ Beat the cream cheese, ¼ cup sugar, egg and 1 teaspoon vanilla in a mixer bowl until blended. Spread over the prepared layer.

◆ Combine the apples and lemon juice in a bowl, tossing to coat. Add ⅓ cup sugar, 2 teaspoons flour, cinnamon and almonds, mixing until the fruit is coated evenly. Spoon over the prepared layers.

◆ Bake at 450 degrees for 10 minutes. Reduce the oven temperature to 400 degrees.

◆ Bake for 25 minutes longer.

◆ Makes 12 to 16 servings.

Saragli or Baklava Pinwheels

½ cup sugar

½ cup water

1 cup Greek honey

12 ounces blanched almonds, lightly toasted, finely chopped

12 ounces natural pistachios, finely chopped

⅔ cup sugar

2 to 3 teaspoons grated lemon peel

2 teaspoons cinnamon

1 pound phyllo pastry

2 cups clarified unsalted butter

Chopped pistachios

◆ Combine the ½ cup sugar and water in a saucepan. Bring to a boil. Boil until clear; reduce heat. Stir in the honey.

◆ Simmer for 3 to 5 minutes, stirring occasionally. Let stand until cool.

◆ Combine the almonds, 12 ounces pistachios, ⅔ cup sugar, lemon peel and cinnamon in a bowl and mix well.

◆ Lay 1 sheet of the phyllo pastry on work surface, leaving the remaining pastry covered with a damp cloth to prevent drying out. Brush with some of the butter. Fold crosswise into half and brush with butter. Lay another phyllo sheet on top so that half of it covers the folded sheet. Brush with butter and sprinkle with some of the almond mixture. Fold to enclose the filling and butter. Repeat the stacking process with 6 more phyllo sheets, butter and almond mixture.

◆ Fold in 1 inch on the long side to secure the almond mixture. Roll, using jelly roll technique, starting on the opposite long side. Cut into ½- to ¾-inch slices. Arrange on a lightly greased baking sheet. Repeat the process with the remaining phyllo, butter and almond mixture.

◆ Bake at 350 degrees for 25 minutes or until golden brown.

◆ Pour the cooled syrup over the hot pastries. Spoon chopped pistachios in the center of each pinwheel just before serving.

◆ Makes variable servings.

Chocolate Mint Cheesecake

*2 cups chocolate wafer
crumbs*

*2 tablespoons melted
margarine*

⅛ teaspoon cinnamon

*2 pounds cream cheese,
softened*

1 cup sugar

4 eggs

*2¾ tablespoons green crème
de menthe*

*¼ teaspoon peppermint
extract*

¼ teaspoon salt

*½ cup semisweet chocolate
chips*

◆ Combine the wafer crumbs, margarine and cinnamon in a bowl and mix well. Pat over the bottom of a greased and floured 9-inch springform pan.

◆ Beat the cream cheese and sugar in a mixer bowl until blended. Add the eggs, beating until smooth. Beat in the crème de menthe, peppermint flavoring and salt.

◆ Spoon into the prepared pan. Sprinkle with the chocolate chips, stirring gently to incorporate.

◆ Bake at 325 degrees for 45 minutes. Turn off oven.

◆ Let stand in oven with door closed for 1 hour.

◆ Chill until serving time. Remove the side of the pan. Transfer the cheesecake to a cake plate. Cut into slices.

◆ Makes 8 to 10 servings.

*In 1834, horse-powered
street cars came to
Buffalo.*

Cranberry Ice

Serve as a side dish or in between courses to cleanse the palate.

1 quart fresh cranberries

2 cups water

1 cup sugar

Juice of 2 oranges

Juice of 1 lemon

1 teaspoon grated orange zest

1 egg white, stiffly beaten

Stiffly beaten egg whites are beaten until peaks stand up straight but remain moist and glossy. They hold air, which expands when heated. Soft peaks droop a bit.

◆ Combine the cranberries and water in a saucepan. Cook until the cranberries are tender. Stir in the sugar.

◆ Press the mixture through a sieve, discarding the skins.

◆ Combine the pulp, orange juice, lemon juice and orange zest in a bowl and mix well. Spoon into a 9x13-inch dish.

◆ Freeze, covered, until firm. Stir in the egg white; the mixture should be smooth and pink.

◆ Freeze, covered, until firm.

◆ Makes 10 to 12 servings.

In 1910, the Stoddart Brothers Drug Store in Buffalo created the ice cream sundae.

Quaker Bonnet Mousse Glacé

4 cups whipping cream

1 cup baking cocoa

¾ cup confectioners' sugar

2 tablespoons dark rum

1 Heath bar, finely ground

◆ Chill a mixer bowl and beaters.

◆ Combine the whipping cream, baking cocoa, confectioners' sugar and rum in the chilled mixer bowl.

◆ Beat at low speed with chilled beaters. Beat at high speed until stiff peaks form, scraping the bowl occasionally; do not overbeat. Spoon into a serving bowl; sprinkle with the candy bar.

◆ May serve immediately or freeze in a round dish and cut into wedges.

◆ Makes 10 to 12 servings.

More Than Mom's Bread Pudding

*1 loaf slightly dry French
   bread*

1 cup raisins

Rum or bourbon

4 cups milk

1 cup sugar

½ cup packed brown sugar

*1 cup chopped walnuts or
   pecans*

1 cup shredded coconut

3 tablespoons melted butter

*2 tablespoons vanilla
   extract*

4 eggs, beaten

Rum Sauce (below)

◆ Cut the bread into 6 to 8 cups of cubes. Dry at room temperature for a few days or in a slow oven for a short time. Plump the raisins in rum or bourbon if desired.

◆ Combine the milk, sugar, brown sugar, raisins, walnuts, coconut, butter, vanilla and eggs in a bowl and mix well. Add the bread cubes and mix gently.

◆ Let stand until the milk is absorbed. May add additional milk if needed for moist cubes. Pour into a buttered 9x12-inch baking dish.

◆ Bake at 350 degrees for 1½ hours. Serve warm or cold with Rum Sauce.

◆ Makes 12 to 15 servings.

Rum Sauce

1 cup confectioners' sugar

½ cup butter

½ egg yolk

½ cup rum or bourbon

◆ Combine the confectioners' sugar and butter in a saucepan.

◆ Cook until blended, stirring constantly. Stir in the egg yolk. Add the rum gradually, stirring constantly.

◆ Cook until heated through, stirring frequently.

◆ Makes 1½ cups.

Raspberry Torte

1¼ cups sifted flour

¼ cup sugar

¼ teaspoon salt

1 cup butter or margarine,
   softened

1 cup sugar

3 tablespoons cornstarch

20 ounces frozen
   raspberries

45 large marshmallows

1 cup milk

1 cup whipping cream,
   whipped

———◆———

*Cutting in refers to
the process of mixing
shortening, butter, or
margarine with dry
ingredients using a
pastry blender, knife,
or fork to produce a
crumbly mixture.*

◆ Combine the flour, ¼ cup sugar and salt in a bowl and mix well. Cut in the butter until crumbly. Pat over the bottom of a 9x13-inch baking pan.

◆ Bake at 350 degrees for 15 to 18 minutes or until light brown.

◆ Remove to a wire rack to cool.

◆ Combine 1 cup sugar and cornstarch in a saucepan and mix well. Add the raspberries. Bring to a boil, stirring constantly.

◆ Boil until thickened, stirring constantly. Cool slightly. Spoon over the baked layer.

◆ Chill in the refrigerator.

◆ Combine the marshmallows and milk in a saucepan.

◆ Cook over low heat until blended, stirring constantly. Remove from heat. Fold in the whipped cream. Spread over the prepared layers.

◆ Chill until serving time.

◆ Makes 12 to 15 servings.

Italian Rum Custard Strawberry Trifle

6 eggs, beaten

¾ cup sugar

¼ teaspoon salt

1¼ cups flour

½ cup sugar

½ cup cornstarch

½ teaspoon salt

3½ cups milk

2 egg yolks

2 tablespoons butter, cut
    into 8 pieces

2 teaspoons vanilla extract

◆ Beat the eggs until frothy. Add ¾ cup sugar 2 tablespoons at a time, beating well after each addition.

◆ Beat for 3 minutes longer, scraping the bowl occasionally. Add ¼ teaspoon salt, beating constantly until mixed.

◆ Sift ⅓ of the flour over the egg mixture and fold in. Repeat the process until all the flour has been incorporated. Pour into a 9-inch greased and floured springform pan.

◆ Bake at 350 degrees for 40 minutes or until the cake tests done.

◆ Cool in the pan on a wire rack for 10 minutes. Loosen the cake from the side of the pan with a sharp knife; remove the side of the pan. Remove the cake to a wire rack to cool completely.

◆ Combine ½ cup sugar, cornstarch and ½ teaspoon salt in a saucepan. Whisk in the milk gradually. Bring to a boil over medium heat, stirring constantly. Boil for 3 minutes, stirring constantly. Remove from heat.

◆ Whisk the egg yolks in a bowl. Stir in 1 cup of the hot milk mixture, whisking constantly. Whisk the egg yolk mixture into the hot milk mixture.

◆ Cook over low heat for 1 minute, stirring constantly. Pour into a medium bowl. Add the butter, stirring until melted. Stir in the vanilla. Press waxed paper onto the surface of the custard.

◆ Cool slightly. Chill in the refrigerator.

Assembling Trifle:

4 cups whipping cream

2 teaspoons unflavored
   gelatin

¼ cup confectioners' sugar

2 pints fresh strawberries

6 to 9 tablespoons dark rum

---

*Confectioners' sugar is
a fine powdery sugar
made by grinding and
sifting granulated sugar.
Frequently a small amount
of cornstarch is added to
prevent caking.*

◆ Pour the whipping cream into a mixer bowl. Sprinkle with the gelatin. Stir in the confectioners' sugar. Beat until stiff peaks form. Chill, covered, in the refrigerator.

◆ Reserve 11 whole strawberries with stems and chill. Cut the remaining strawberries into thin slices.

◆ Cut the cooled cake horizontally into 3 equal layers. Brush the top of each layer with 2 to 3 tablespoons of the rum. Cut each layer into 1x2-inch fingers.

◆ Reserve ¼ of the whipped cream.

◆ Arrange the cake fingers from 1 layer in the bottom of a trifle bowl or glass bowl with straight sides. Layer with ⅓ of the custard and half the strawberries. Arrange some cake fingers around the edge. Spread the strawberries with ⅓ of the remaining whipped cream. Repeat the process with another layer of cake fingers, ⅓ of the custard, the remaining strawberries and another ⅓ of the whipped cream. Top with the remaining cake fingers, the remaining custard and remaining whipped cream.

◆ Chill for 8 hours or longer. Pipe the reserved whipped cream into rosettes over the top of the trifle. Arrange 10 of the reserved strawberries around the edge and 1 in the center.

◆ Makes 10 servings.

My Private Tiramisù

1 cup cold espresso

2 tablespoons dark rum

1 tablespoon sugar

1 tablespoon crème de cacao

1 pound mascarpone cheese

¼ cup dark rum

2 tablespoons vanilla extract

1 tablespoon lemon juice

1 cup whipping cream

1 tablespoon confectioners' sugar

4 egg yolks

½ cup sugar

4 egg whites, stiffly beaten

24 ladyfingers

6 ounces bittersweet chocolate, grated

Chocolate-covered espresso beans

◆ Combine the espresso, 2 tablespoons dark rum, 1 tablespoon sugar and crème de cacao in a bowl and mix well.

◆ Combine the mascarpone cheese, ¼ cup dark rum, vanilla and lemon juice in a bowl and mix well.

◆ Beat the whipping cream with the confectioners' sugar in a mixer bowl. Fold into the mascarpone cheese mixture.

◆ Beat the egg yolks and ½ cup sugar in a mixer bowl until thickened. Stir into the mascarpone cheese mixture. Fold in the egg whites.

◆ Dip the ladyfingers into the espresso mixture. Layer the ladyfingers, cheese mixture and grated chocolate ⅓ at a time in a trifle bowl. Sprinkle with espresso beans.

◆ Chill until set.

◆ Makes 10 to 12 servings.

Special Thanks

The Junior League of Buffalo extends it's sincere and deep appreciation and gratitude to Margaret M. Martin, AWS, for the donation of her creative watercolors; which portray the essence of Buffalo and it's surrounding environs.

Albright-Knox Art Gallery—Karen Spaulding

Allentown Village Society, Inc.—Mary Myszkiewicz, President

The Bon Ton Stores, Inc.

Botanical Gardens—Susan Ruh

Buckley, Thorne, Messina, McDermott & Associates, Inc.

The Buffalo Club—Marleen Safsinclli

Buffalo Place, Inc.

Business First—Donna Collins

City of Buffalo Community Development Office

Friendship Festival—Tracey LeBlonk

Glidden Machine & Tool

The Junior League of Buffalo, Inc. Board of Directors
1994–1995, 1995–1996, and 1996–1997

Waldenbooks—Colleen Banks,
District Community Relations Coordinator

Western New York Warcs, Inc., Meyer Enterprises—
Brian Meyer

and
especially our wonderful families

Individual Patrons

G. Clifford Abromats and Janice Worobec

Isabelle Spurr Appleton

Belmore Bridgford

Carl, Debbie and Craig Bucki

Mr. and Mrs. Robert E. Deemer

Mr. and Mrs. Robert Farrell

Barbara Galvin

Mr. and Mrs. James Gresens

John and Carol Grieco

Virginia Harrington

Emerson and Peggy Horner

Dr. and Mrs. Edwin Jenis

Mrs. Benjamin C. Johnson

Mary Ann Kresse

Mrs. Walter S. de la Plante

Gretchen Engstrom Stringer

Margaret Toohey

Christina Willis

Corporate Patrons

Delaware North Companies Incorporated

Jameson Roofing

Advantage Beauty and Barber Supply

Capello Salons and Day Spa

Chase Manhattan Bank, N.A.

Community Pet Care

Laura's Lily Patch

Marlin Arts

Media Play

Quaker Bonnet

Rich Products Corporation

Selective Insurance

Silk Flowers by Lady Gloria

Suzn O'

Cookbook Committee

Chair
Michelle Murray Alexander

Co-Chair
Barbara Bielecki

Sustainer Co-Chair
Marsha Gresens

Secretary
Donna Farrell

Marketing Co-Chairs
Julie Skinner
Renata Szirmai

Recipe Co-Chairs
Marcy Denzak
Mary Schuler

Editorial Chair
Jennifer Gerace

Editorial Sustainer Chair
Noreen Falkner

Production & Design Chair
Sharon Grandoni

*Production & Design Sustainer
   Chair*
Elizabeth S. R. Hirsch

Placement Committee
Trish Barrick-Wright
Karen Bruch
Heidi Conschafter
Mary Dewey
Sarah Hausherr
Peggy Horner
Lynn Newiger
Beth Nichols
Kathleen Peoples Riker
Wendy Sanders
Janice Worobec

Grazing Gourmet Committee
Jayne Carter Farkas
Mollie Gaughan Hill
Mary Lou Whelan

Support Committee
Elizabeth Angelbeck
Mary Jo Carroll
Jackie Goergen
Jutta Helm
Cynthia Horrigan
Elaine Lydon
Cherie Messore
Tina Nantka
Lisa Nolan
Carol Sibick
Anne Slater
Susan Urlaub
Patty Yanity

Culinary Sources

Restaurants

Creekview Restaurant
David Schutte, Owner
Lobster Ginger

The Garden Restaurant of
The Albright-Knox Art Gallery
Chef Dan Reisch
*Cold Green Tomato Soup with
    Black Truffle*

The Grille on Walden
Sheraton Inn
Menzo Palmer
Steak Shaniqua

The Hourglass Restaurant
Pastry Chef Eras Bechakas
*Apple Crisp with Lemon Honey
    Cream*
Pear and Ginger Brown Butter Tart
Saragli or Baklava Pinwheels

Hutch's Restaurant
Chef/Owner Mark Hutchinson
Jambalaya Pasta

Just Pasta
Donald Warfe, Owner
*Rotini with Chicken, Gorgonzola
    Cheese and Peas*

Lord Chumley's
*Cold Vichyssoise or Hot Potato
    and Leek Soup*

Oliver's Restaurant
Chef Michael Andrzejewski
*Barbecued Duck Breasts on
    Sweet Corn Pancakes*

Pranzo Ristorante
Chef Gene Pigeon
*Linguini with Roasted Yellow
    Pepper Sauce*
Olive Pesto Spread

Shepherd's Pub
Dominic Ruzzine, Owner
*Penne with Mushrooms,
    Tomatoes and Gorgonzola
    Cheese*

Transit Valley Country Club
Chef Mark Wright
Fillets of Sole Sauté
Seafood Sauce

Food Establishments

Guercio's
Santina Guerico
*Tomato and Mozzarella Pasta
    Salad*

Premier Gourmet
Broccoli Slaw

Quaker Bonnet
Chef/Owner Liz Kolken
Quaker Bonnet Lemon Angel Pies
Quaker Bonnet Mousse Glaceé

Vito's Gourmet Market, Inc.
Chef/Owner Mary Joy Buscemi
M. J.'s Stuffed Pumpkins

Chefs

Chef Steven Bogart
Szechwan-Style Cucumbers

Chef Merle Ellis
Curry-Glazed Sesame Wings
Gingered Chicken Wings
Chinese Fried Chicken Wings

Chef Wm. R. Ott
Chicken Pesto Pizza

Contributors

The Junior League of Buffalo expresses grateful appreciation to those contributors who spent countless hours and/or dollars to provide us with the quality recipes featured in *Great Lake Effects*. We deeply regret that we were unable to include all of the recipes submitted due to space limitations. We hope we have not inadvertently excluded anyone from the following list:

Annie Adams	Diana Borja	Donna Collins
Herb Alexander	Terri Boubaris	Mary Sue Collins
Michelle M. Alexander	Wendy Bowers	Rebecca Collins
Nicole Ambarchian	Jeri Boyland	Madonna Comerate
Jean Ambrose	Karen Bristol	Joanne Conboy
Liz Angelbeck	Sally Broad	Kathleen Conboy
Tom Augello	Sandra Broderick	Marcia Conny
Mary Bacon	Jill Bronsky	Dilara Constantine
Judi Bainbridge	Karen Bruch	Sumiko Corley Moots
Diana Baiocchi	Deborah Bruch Bucki	Mary Jo Cornell
Marilyn Baiocchi	Daniel Buckley	Ann Craig
Robert Baiocchi	Karen Bulner	Eileen Daetsch
Margaret Ballou	Judi Bunge	Robert Davis
Mary Barger	Nemia Burgess	Clotilde Dedecker
Rita Barger	Terry Burnham Jenis	Sherry Deemer
Andrea Barke-Harris	Tory Burnham Jenis	Harold DeNicola
Ruth Barone	Susan Burns	Sharon DeNicola
Mary Beth Barrett	Christine Buscaglia	Deborah Dennis Young
Mary Louise Barrett	Nancy Buscaglia	Susan Dentinger
Tricia Barrick-Wright	Betty Marie Calandra	Marcy Denzak
Gayle Barton	Aubrey Calhoun	Florence Dewey
Kathleen Bates	Naomi Calieri	Mary Dewey
Sheila Battle	Josie Capuana	Tricia Di'Fato
Gail Bauser	Eileen Cardinal	Lucille DiFiglia
Sawrie Becker	Amy L. Carpenter	Cynthia Dobbertean
Ann Bell	Jayne Carter Farkas	Cathleen Doeblin
Laura Benedetti	Susan Cason	Tracy Drury
Marco Benedetti	Suzanne Celeste	Mary Grace Duggan
Arlene Bensen	Melissa Chelius	Bridgette Dukarm
Jennifer Berke	Nancy Cheyney	Luci Dzurilla
Sherrie Bernat	Kathleen Chmura	Laura Ehret
Kara Beutel	Mary Christiano	Lucille Emmi
Barbara Bielecki	Gloria Clark	Lynn Endres
Debbie Bieler	Steven Cline	Lynn Engle
Ann Bischof	Emily Coassin	Michael Essrow
Lisa Bonaventura	Mary Coffee	Sherri Evchick
Dee Dee Booth	Michele Cofield	Noreen Falkner

Donna Farrell
Lisa Faturos
Jill Fink
Barbara Fitch
Sarajane Fletcher
John Foster
Theresa Foster
Annemarie Franczyk
Dawn Frazita
Sylvia Fredricks
Sonia Freedlander
Elaine Friedhaber
Rosemary Gabrielson
Nan Gallivan
Nancy M. Garrison
Mary George
Jackie Georgen
Jennifer Gerace
Marcia Gerace
Amy Gernold
Carol Gernold
Joanne Gettleman
Cindy Getz
Nancy Giardino
Elisabeth C. Giese
Brenda Giroux
Mary M. Gisel
Laura Glass
Jackie Goergen
Flo Goeseke
Marc Golda
Mary Good
Linda Gordon
Nina Gordon
Hope Gower
Joan Grandoni
Sharon Grandoni
Cecelia Grasser
Mary Greer
Marsha Gresens
Mary Gresham, Ph.D.
Margaret Griffin
Sylvia Gugino
Judy Harvey

Mary Hausherr
Sarah Hausherr
Renee Hayman
Julie Hazzan
Judith S. Hedding
Bonnie Heidorf
Melanie Henderson
Christine Hentz
Ginger Heussler
Mollie Gaughan Hill
Trish Hodan
Margie Holcombe
Ginny Hollum
Peggy Horner
Cynthia Horrigan
Valencia Hoven
Elizabeth Howard
Mary Jane Howard
Ellen Hughes
Martie Hughes
Mary Jo Hunt
Mary Hyde
Alice Jacobs
Caryn Jarmusz
Cathy Jarmusz
Theresa Jehle
Kim Johnsen
Mary Johnson
Shirley Joya
Dana Juhasz
Lisa Kaempf
Nancy Knight
Kristin Koessler
MaryAnn Kresse
Joanne Lara
Leila Laspisa
Lynette Laspisa-
  Baiocco
Barbara Leisner
Denise Levy
Ann Lewis
Trish Lewis
Carol Litfin
Jevene Littlewood

Elaine Lydon
Jennifer Lyons Greco
Maureen Macaulay
Susan MacPherson
Suzanne Mahoney
Joan M. Maitino
Margaret Maloney
Martha Mangan
Debby Marinaccio
Laurel Dana Mark
Lisa Markarian
Lorrie Mattar
Linda Matusiak
Nancy Mayer
Carol Mayian
Marge Shea McBurney
Joan McGuire
Susan McHugh
Karen Russo
  McLaughlin
MaryAnne McMahon
Diane McMullen
Jessie Melson
Francesca Messiah
Cherie Messore
Rita Messore
Marie Metz
Cindy Meyer
Carolyn Miller
Donald Miller
Kathy Miller
Linda Miller
Pamela Mills
Eileen Monomakhoff
Kathleen
  Monomakhoff Loree
Angela Moscicki
Suzanne Moule
  Hettrick
Jeannie Mullan
Doris Murphy
MaryAnn Murphy
Sally Murphy Woods
Teresa Murphy

Jane S. Murray
Karen Murrett
Tina Nantka
Doreen Newiger
Lynn Newiger
Beth Nichols
Lisa Nolan
Lynn Nowak
Heidi Nuchereno
Julie Oberlies
Patty O'Brien
Laurette O'Connor
   Regan
Gretchen O'Donnell
Caroline Ogiony
Rose Olds
Laurie Olivia
Paula Orlowski
Concetta Ortolano
Patricia Papademetriou
Becky Pappas
Margarita Pareja
Mary Beth Parrinello
Linda McCain-Parson
Dean Penman
Libbie Penman
Erin M. Peradotto
Lisa Perrine
Stephanie Pfalzgraf
Janet Phillips
Margaret Phillips
Paula Pirson
Sandy Pirson
Susan Poole
Ann Posner
Patricia Prior
Ann Quackenbush
Lu Quimby
Kathleen H. Radetich
Sharon Raymond
Joyce Redlin
Maureen Redlin
Shelly Reidy

Lorey Repicci
Julienne Ricchaizzi
Kathleen Peoples
   Riker
Mary Rizzo
Pat Roberts
Kathleen Rose
Maureen Rose
Cheryl Rossi
Rose Rucci
Patricia Ruh
Frances Russell
Mary Rutecki
Maureen Rutecki
Leslie Salomon
Betsy Sanders
Jean Sheila Sanders
Wendy Sanders
Josie Sarac
Maria Schory
Mary Schuler
Kim Scott
Cindy Seigle
Colleen Seminara
Joanne Seminara
Suzy Shallowhorn
Patricia Shine
Susan Siegel
Beth Simons
JoAnne Skaros
Julie Skinner
Virginia Skinner
Anne Slater
Deidre Slowinski
Sarah Smith
Kathy Smolka
Ricia Spellman
Ellen Stanford
Mary Louise Stanley
Jo Anne Stubbs
Elaine Suarez
Kevin Sullivan
Monica Summers

Elisabeth Szirmai
Renata Szirmai
Rita Szkatulski
Linda Tague
Connie Cline
   Tambacas
Peter Tambacas
Kathleen Tank
Carrie Telford
Amy Thomas
Jane Alice Tom
Nan Tomani
Sherleen Tomasello
Barbara Tomasi
Margy Toohey
Laura Tucker
Linda Ungaro
Susan Urlaub
Theresa Vallone
Elizabeth Vogel
Valerie Voisard
Elizabeth Vossler
Maureen Walsh
Barb Weaver
Gary Weber
Lisa Weltzer
Margaret Whalen
   Brechtel
Mary Lou Whelan
Kathie Whistler
Ann White
Ellen Willett
Randi Wilson
Kathleen Wilson-Ward
Amy Wisner
Blaine Witt
Janice Worobec
Trudy Wythe
Janet Yavener
Darcy Zacher
Cheryl Zimmerman
Patricia Zimmerman
Julie Zulewski

Bibliography

Bisco, Jim. *A Greater Look at Greater Buffalo*. USA: Windsor
Publications, Inc., 1986.

Brown, Richard C., and Bob Watson. *Buffalo: Lake City in Niagara
Land*. USA: Windsor Publications, Inc., 1981.

Fox, Austin M. *Designated Landmarks of the Niagara Frontier*. Buffalo,
New York: Meyer Enterprises, 1986.

Glaser, Kenncth, Jack Messmer, and Paul Redding. *Waterview Guide to
Buffalo Harbor*. Buffalo, New York: The Lower Lakes Marine
Historical Society and the Western New York Heritage Institute, 1989.

Sheridan, Jan, et al. *Buffalo Treasures: A Downtown Walking Guide*.
Buffalo, New York: Western New York Wares, Inc., 1995.

Vogel, Michael N., and Paul F. Redding. *Maritime Buffalo*. Buffalo, New
York: The Western New York Heritage Institute, 1990.

Metric Equivalents

Although the United States has opted to postpone converting to metric measurements, most other countries, including England and Canada, use the metric system. The following chart provides convenient approximate equivalents for allowing use of regular kitchen measures when cooking from foreign recipes.

Volume

*These metric measures are approximate
benchmarks for purposes of home food preparation.
1 milliliter = 1 cubic centimeter = 1 gram*

Liquid	Dry
1 teaspoon = 5 milliliters	1 quart = 1 liter
1 tablespoon = 15 milliliters	1 ounce = 30 grams
1 fluid ounce = 30 milliliters	1 pound = 450 grams
1 cup = 250 milliliters	2.2 pounds = 1 kilogram
1 pint = 500 milliliters	

Weight

1 ounce = 28 grams
1 pound = 450 grams

Length

1 inch = $2^{1}/_{2}$ centimeters
$^{1}/_{16}$ inch = 1 millimeter

Formulas Using Conversion Factors

*When approximate conversions are not accurate enough, use these
formulas to convert measures from one system to another.*

Measurements	Formulas
ounces to grams:	# ounces x 28.3 = # grams
grams to ounces:	# grams x 0.035 = # ounces
pounds to grams:	# pounds x 453.6 = # grams
pounds to kilograms:	# pounds x 0.45 = # kilograms
ounces to milliliters:	# ounces x 30 = # milliliters
cups to liters:	# cups x 0.24 = # liters
inches to centimeters:	# inches x 2.54 = # centimeters
centimeters to inches:	# centimeters x 0.39 = # inches

Metric Equivalents

Approximate Weight to Volume

Some ingredients which we commonly measure by volume are measured by weight in foreign recipes. Here are a few examples for easy reference.

flour, all-purpose, unsifted	1 pound = 450 grams = $3^1/_2$ cups
flour, all-purpose, sifted	1 pound = 450 grams = 4 cups
sugar, granulated	1 pound = 450 grams = 2 cups
sugar, brown, packed	1 pound = 450 grams = $2^1/_4$ cups
sugar, confectioners'	1 pound = 450 grams = 4 cups
sugar, confectioners', sifted	1 pound = 450 grams = $4^1/_2$ cups
butter	1 pound = 450 grams = 2 cups

Temperature

Remember that foreign recipes frequently express temperatures in Centigrade rather than Fahrenheit.

Temperatures	Fahrenheit	Centigrade
room temperature	68°	20°
water boils	212°	100°
baking temperature	350°	177°
baking temperature	375°	190.5°
baking temperature	400°	204.4°
baking temperature	425°	218.3°
baking temperature	450°	232°

Use the following formulas when temperature conversions are necessary.

Centigrade degrees x $^9/_5$ + 32 = Fahrenheit degrees

Fahrenheit degrees - 32 x $^5/_9$ = Centigrade degrees

American Measurement Equivalents

1 tablespoon = 3 teaspoons	12 tablespoons = $^3/_4$ cup
2 tablespoons = 1 ounce	16 tablespoons = 1 cup
4 tablespoons = $^1/_4$ cup	1 cup = 8 ounces
5 tablespoons + 1 teaspoon = $^1/_3$ cup	2 cups = 1 pint
	4 cups = 1 quart
8 tablespoons = $^1/_2$ cup	4 quarts = 1 gallon

Index

For additional copies of
Great Lake Effects
send $18.95 plus $3.50
shipping and handling
for each book

to:

The Junior League of
Buffalo, Inc.
45 Elmwood Avenue
Buffalo, New York 14201

Checks, money orders,
MasterCard and Visa accepted.

Credit card orders please
include name as printed on
card, account number and
expiration date

or

call 716-882-7520.

About Buffalo

And much more . . .